TIME'S UP

The Prophecies of Daniel
Unsealed for Today's Teen

MELISSA HANSON

TIME'S UP: THE PROPHECIES OF DANIEL UNSEALED FOR TODAY'S TEEN

THIS BOOK IS DEDICATED TO
THE YOUTH WHO WANT THEIR
LIVES TO MAKE AN ETERNAL
DIFFERENCE FOR CHRIST
IN TODAY'S WORLD.

CONTENTS

THE PARABLE OF DOOMSDAY PREACHER JOE

"Do not seal the words of the prophecy
of this book, for the time is at hand."

(Rev. 22:10)

Now the word of the Lord came to Joe, a Christian teenager living in the last days of Earth's history, saying, "Get up and share the prophecies in My Word because the world is wicked, and I'm about to come back!"

The last thing young Joe wanted to do was preach an unpopular message that might make him look bad in front of all his friends. So the Lord gave the same message to other young people, but none would wake up from their spiritual sleep and do anything about it!

Needless to say, the Lord was unhappy with Joe and his church buddies and allowed troublesome times to come upon them.

Meanwhile, some of the lost were afraid of what was happening in the world, and they begged God to explain the Bible's prophecies and how they applied to their lives. And since they had heard that Joe and his church had great knowledge about the prophecies in the book of Daniel, they shook him awake and cried, "Why are you sleeping in such a time as this? Wake up and tell us what we can do to be saved! We have gone from one place to another, trying to find out about Christ's second coming, but all

1

we know is what we have learned from watching the "Left Behind" movies on TV. Please tell us why all these bad things are happening to us! Aren't you a Christian who has been taught Bible prophecy? Why are you not sharing its messages so we can all be saved?"

Unfortunately, Joe replied, "Yes, I suppose I should share what I know about the Bible, but I'm kind of rusty on the prophecies, especially the ones in Daniel! It's been a long time since I have studied them. But I can tell you all about grace! I just don't want to scare anyone with all those symbols of wild beasts or their meanings for us today. I certainly don't want to be accused of judging people!"

Then the lost who had admitted their hopeless condition were angry because they realized that their only chance of understanding God's prophecies was gone if Joe didn't tell them. So, they desperately prayed that the Lord would not hold them responsible for not knowing what Joe didn't care to share.

Now God heard these honest souls' cries and allowed double trouble to fall upon Joe and his church because of their unfaithfulness to the Lord's special calling. And Joe cried out from the belly of despair, begging God to forgive his disobedience in keeping the Bible's truth all to himself! So, the Lord had mercy upon Joe and his church and gave them another opportunity to warn the world of His soon return.

And God said again, "Get up and go tell the world about the prophecies in the book of Daniel. I will help you explain them clearly so that everyone will be able to understand!"

So, this time, Joe obeyed, although he was still reluctant to share a message of the world's soon destruction when his friends

2

were going "green" to save the earth. However, guilt and fear of further trouble impelled him to cry, "The Lord says that the world is in big trouble because it has forsaken the Lord and the commandments of His Word!"

And the people listened—and many repented—which dismayed and dumbfounded poor Joe! He had never expected such a turn of events because many claimed that preaching Bible prophecy didn't work in modern times. What should he do now? Having done his religious duty, Joe quickly left and went back home where he could escape the tedious task of answering a bombardment of questions from the crowds.

Feeling overwhelmed, Joe had time to ponder his perplexing success. What would all his friends at church think when they heard what he had done? Who would want to hang out with Doomsday Preacher Joe? He just wished that God would free him of his special calling and allow him to go back to his easy lifestyle of watching TV, checking his social media, and playing video games!

However, the Lord did not give up! He continued to plead with Joe and His church to share the truths of Bible prophecy with the world before it was too late...

***

With whom in this modern parable of Jonah can you relate most? Are you like Joe, who had much biblical knowledge but was afraid to share it with others? Or do you relate more to the crowd, who was trying to make sense of what was happening in the world and longing for answers found only in the Bible? Either way, the Holy Spirit promises understanding and the ability to distinguish truth from error: "… when He, the Spirit of truth has come, He will guide you into all truth ... and He will tell you things to come" (John 16:13). You don't need to be a scholar! Just have faith and ask, and the Lord will explain how His Word applies to YOUR life today! So don't be afraid and hesitate like Joe because the amazing prophecies of Daniel are about to be unsealed before your very eyes!

THE WORST NIGHTMARE IN HISTORY

"Surely the Lord God does nothing, un-
less He reveals His secret to His servants
the prophets."

(Amos 3:7)

Have you ever had a nightmare that scared you to death? Did you wake up breathing hard with your heart pounding in your chest and sweat pouring down your forehead? You are not the only one who has had a nightmare! Surprisingly, about half of children between the ages of three and six, and twenty percent of children ages six to twelve report frequent nightmares.[1] Additionally, in the general population, one out of twenty people have nightmares every week.[2] So probably everyone has had a scary dream at some time in his or her life!

A King's Nightmare

A similar terrifying experience happened to a king in the Bible who lived long ago. His name was Nebuchadnezzar, and when he awoke from his nightmare, he was so shaken that he couldn't even remember it (or, at least, that is what he claimed!). So he summoned his magicians and wisemen and demanded that *they* tell him his dream and the meaning of it. If they didn't, they would be

---

[1] https://www.sleepfoundation.org/nightmares/nightmares-in-children

[2] https://www.psychologytoday.com/us/blog/the-red-light-district/201906/15-frightful-facts-about-nightmares

killed! Why would King Nebuchadnezzar be so upset about not knowing the meaning of a nightmare? Back then, many believed that dreams were given by the gods and were very important messages about the future. Perhaps that's why he might have been so worried!

But how do you think his wisemen must have felt? The king's nightmare had become their reality! What might you have done if you had been in their place? They probably wanted to run away and hide! Unfortunately, however, there was no chance of escape! Because the king did not tell his counselors the dream, they could not make up any interpretations. Hopelessly, they declared, "No man on earth can tell you your dream. Only the gods know!" Unfortunately, this response just made the king madder! Immediately, he demanded that all his wisemen be killed!

Daniel's Destiny

Not knowing anything about Nebuchadnezzar's decree, Daniel, one of the king's wisemen, awoke to the sound of beating on his front door. Memories of his brutal arrest as a young teenager and his long trek to Babylon swept through Daniel's mind at the sound of the insistent knocking. Back home in Jerusalem, he had been a Jewish prince, a part of the royal family, but tragically, he had been captured and forced to be King Nebuchadnezzar's servant. However, the God of Heaven had not forsaken him! The Lord had given him so much wisdom that the king had made him a part of his special council of wisemen.

But now, Daniel's heartbeat quickened as he opened the door — only to discover soldiers waiting to take him to his execution! *Why?* Sweat began to form on Daniel's brow. His hands shook uncontrollably. *Why was the king so angry?* The soldiers told him about the nightmare and how his fellow wisemen had been unable to tell the king his dream or its interpretation. Because of this, all the court's counselors and wisemen had been sentenced to death.

Daniel's mind must have raced... if only the king would give him some time! He knew that his God was able to tell him the king's dream and its interpretation. But would he even have a chance to ask his friends to pray with him and petition the Lord?

Begging to plead his case before the king, Daniel was taken to the palace. With a pounding heart, he bowed before Nebuchadnezzar and humbly asked him for time to pray so that His God could show him the dream and its interpretation. To his relief, the king reluctantly agreed.

A Prayer and a Praise

Immediately, Daniel left the palace and went straight to his three trusted friends, explaining the urgency of the situation. All of them fervently prayed together. That night, the Lord answered their prayer by revealing the king's dream and its meaning to Daniel. The next morning, full of awe at God's mercy, Daniel stood before Nebuchadnezzar and declared:

> You, O king, were watching; and behold, a great image! This great image, whose splendor was excellent, stood before you; and its form was awesome. This image's head was of fine gold, its chest and arms of silver, its belly and thighs of bronze, its legs of iron, its feet partly of iron and partly of clay. You watched while a stone was cut out without hands, which struck the image on its feet of iron and clay, and broke them in pieces. Then the iron, the clay, the bronze, the silver, and the gold were crushed together... the wind carried them away so that no trace of them was found. And the stone that struck the image became a great mountain and filled the whole earth. (Daniel 2:31-35)

Nebuchadnezzar's face transformed from irritation to amazement! Obviously, Daniel's God had revealed the secret of his dream! The king remembered each detail of the nightmare exactly how Daniel had described it! But still, the mystery of its meaning remained! Would this young Hebrew be able to tell him the interpretation of his dream? Nebuchadnezzar took a deep breath and nodded for Daniel to continue...

> You, O king, are a king of kings... you are this head of gold. But after you shall arise another kingdom inferior to yours; then another, a third kingdom of bronze, which shall rule over all the earth. And the fourth kingdom shall be as strong as iron... and like iron that crushes, that kingdom will break in pieces and crush all the others. Whereas you saw the feet and toes, partly of potter's clay and partly of iron, the kingdom shall be divided... so the kingdom shall be partly strong and partly fragile... And in the days of these kings the God of heaven will set up a kingdom which shall never be destroyed... it shall break in pieces and consume all these kingdoms, and it shall stand forever. In as much as you saw that the stone was cut out of the mountain without hands, and that it broke in pieces the iron, the bronze, the clay, the silver, and the gold—the great God has made known to the king what will come to pass after this. (Daniel 2:37-45)

A Dream Come True

Overcome with admiration for Daniel's God, King Nebuchadnezzar bowed down before Daniel and declared, "Truly your God is the God of gods, the Lord of kings, and a revealer of secrets!" (Daniel 2:47). He immediately rewarded Daniel with great gifts and made him a ruler over Babylon, along with his three friends (Dan.

2:48). Because of these young men's faithfulness, the lives of the rest of the wisemen in the kingdom were spared, and the God of Heaven was praised!

History has proven the truth of Nebuchadnezzar's dream, exactly as the Bible predicted. The metals in the statue symbolized God's people under the rule of four world kingdoms throughout history — Babylon (gold), Medo-Persia (silver), Greece (bronze), and Rome (iron); then Rome's political rulership would be divided, but the Roman papacy would regain its power, specifically in the United States (clay [Jer. 18:4, 6; Gal. 3:28-29]), just before Christ's second coming (the stone that crushed the statue [Matt. 21:42-44]).

Today, we are living in the toenails of the statue's iron and clay feet. Even now, the political and spiritual forces are at work in America, warring against God's people. Only the end of Daniel's prophecy has not yet been fulfilled — when the stone crushes the other kingdoms, and Jesus reigns forever!

Just like Nebuchadnezzar, we can be confident the God of Heaven is the "revealer of secrets." He has accurately foretold what would happen throughout history in His Word. Because His prophecies have been fulfilled exactly as predicted, we can trust the Lord with our lives today and in the future! In fact, He promises to turn a king's worst nightmare into the best dream that anyone could ever imagine when He returns to take us home with Him forever!

DISCUSSION QUESTIONS FOR DANIEL 2

1. Why was King Nebuchadnezzar so upset after he had his nightmare? (Daniel 2:1-3)

2. How did the magicians and wisemen respond to the king's demand? Why would their response make the king so furious, given that wisemen were supposed to be able to predict the future? (Daniel 2:4-12)

3. Who was Daniel, and why was he one of the king's wisemen? (Dan. 1:1, 3-6)

4. What did Daniel do when he was told about the king's decree? (Dan. 2:16-18)

5. Why does God give His people prophecies that foretell the future? (Amos 3:7; John 14:29)

6. Who is represented by the head of gold, and what kingdom did he rule? (Dan. 2:37-39)

7. What world kingdoms do the silver, bronze, iron, and clay represent? (Dan. 2:39-42)

8. Where are we living in the statue of time, and why is this important? (Dan. 2:41-43)

9. What part of the king's dream has not yet been fulfilled? Who does the "Stone" symbolize? (Dan. 2:35-36, 44-45; Matt. 21:42-44)

10. What is the king's response to the interpretation of his dream? Why should we trust God with our future today? (Dan. 2:46-47; Heb. 13:5; Matt. 28:20)

FOUR MONSTER BEASTS

"That which has been is what will be.
That which is done is what will be done...
It has already been in ancient times...."

(Ecclesiastes 1:9-10)

Have you ever put a penny into a spiral? The penny whirls faster and faster as it reaches the middle and then—PLOP! It falls into the hole! According to the Bible, humans are living in a giant spiral, spinning in circles, but advancing in time (Eccl. 1:9). History repeats itself and then continues as a giant chain of events. However, instead of the links being all the same size, each link seems to be getting smaller, resulting in the world's history spinning faster and faster—like a penny in a spiral. Amazingly, the prophecies in the Bible, then, remain relevant and can apply to different time periods. For example, in Matthew 24, Jesus told his disciples to watch for the signs of Jerusalem's destruction as well as the signs of His second coming. When Christ stated this prophecy, it predicted events that would take place back then, but His words would have an even deeper significance for us today! The Lord likely repeats this prophecy in the last days of Earth's history because of its great importance.

Daniel's Vision

You might have heard the saying, "What goes around, comes around." That is exactly what happened to the prophet, Daniel!

When he was but a youth, he had interpreted King Nebuchadnezzar's dream that predicted the world's future. Many years later, it was his turn to have his own nightmare! In a dream, he saw the four winds of heaven stirring up the great sea, likely the Mediterranean Sea (Dan. 7:2). Then four mighty beasts rose from the water, each different from the other (Dan. 7:3).

The Lion with Eagles' Wings—King Nebuchadnezzar/Babylon

The first one looked like a lion, but it had wings like an eagle on its back. Suddenly, its wings were plucked off, and the lion stood to its feet like a man, and a man's heart was given to it (Dan. 7:4). Daniel was quite aware that the lion was a symbol of both the king and the kingdom of Babylon since the palace where he lived hosted many mosaic pictures and statues of lions. Interestingly, today, one can actually see a stone lion statue that still stands in Iraq from Daniel's time, along with pictures of lions on the excavated Ishtar Gate, both revealing lions as symbols of this ancient city.[3] God's Word also refers to Babylon as a raging lion in Jeremiah 50:17, "Israel is like scattered sheep: the lions have driven him away… Nebuchadnezzar king of Babylon has broken his bones." Because the Bible records Daniel reading Jeremiah's prophecies, he must have been aware of Babylon's lion symbol (Dan. 9:2). Therefore, both secular history and biblical writings affirm that lions could represent the king or kingdom of Babylon.

Moreover, Daniel likely remembered Nebuchadnezzar's second nightmare, which he had also interpreted years ago. Back then, God had warned this proud king that he would temporarily lose his mind and act like an animal, and that was exactly what happened! The Bible says that Nebuchadnezzar's heart was changed from that of a man to a beast and his hair grew "like

[3] https://en.wikipedia.org/wiki/Lion_of_Babylon_(statue):

https://en.wikipedia.org/wiki/Ishtar_Gate#Ishtar_Gate_and_Processional_Way

eagles' feathers and his nails like birds' claws" (Dan. 4:16, 33). Fortunately, after seven years, God allowed Nebuchadnezzar's sanity to return, and he was given back his rulership of Babylon. So Daniel probably had no trouble identifying King Nebuchadnezzar and his kingdom of Babylon as the representation of a lion with plucked eagle's wings that stood up like a man. Because Daniel knew that the first animal in his vision represented the kingdom of Babylon, it was not difficult for him to conclude that the rest of the beasts in his dream also symbolized world kingdoms that would rule God's people after Babylon's fall (Dan. 7:23).

The Bear with Three Ribs in its Teeth—Medo-Persia

The second beast Daniel saw looked like a bear that had three ribs between its teeth. It was raised up on one side and told to "arise and devour much flesh" (Dan. 7:5). Daniel actually lived to see this prophecy fulfilled when Cyrus, the king of Persia, and his army diverted Babylon's' water flow and seized the city by entering its unlocked gates through its dry riverbed. God had prophesied the way Babylon would fall and called Cyrus *by name* before he was even born! When he was told of this prophecy, Cyrus was so impressed that he ended up granting permission for Jerusalem to be rebuilt, just as the prophet, Isaiah, had foretold (Is. 44:27-28; Ezra 1:2-3). Once again, the Bible proved its accuracy! Today, archeologists have uncovered a clay cylinder that tells a similar account of King Cyrus's life, further adding validity to biblical prophecy.[4]

At the invasion of the Persians, Babylon's head of gold and winged lion kingdom came crashing down! King Cyrus also conquered Lydia and Egypt, in addition to Babylon, signified by the three ribs sticking out of the bear's mouth. Also, similar to the two silver arms in King Nebuchadnezzar's statue, the Medes and the

---

[4] https://www.biblicalarchaeology.org/daily/ancient-cultures/ancient-near-eastern-world/the-cyrus-cylinder/

Persians ruled the world together, but the Persians became more powerful in the end, just like the bear that was raised up on one side in Daniel's dream. Medo-Persia ruled throughout the rest of Daniel's life. However, like Babylon, it was destined to fall, and Alexander the Great from Greece conquered this "bear" kingdom's rule.

The Four-headed Leopard with Four Bird Wings—Greece

The third beast Daniel saw in his dream looked like a four-headed leopard with four bird wings on its back, "and dominion was given to it" (Dan. 7:6). When Greece defeated the kingdom of Medo-Persia, the rulership of God's people switched from Abraham's descendants in the East to the pagan Gentiles of the West. Interestingly, the Bible speaks of a leopard's inability to change its spots as representative of those who try to do good but instead do evil (Jer. 13:23). Perhaps this text may contain a clue why God chose a leopard to symbolize Greece. Alexander was known for his ruthless, cruel conquest of power! He defeated the Medes and Persians with lightning speed, signified by the four bird wings on the leopard's back. Moreover, the "wings" of his kingdom stretched to the four corners of the earth, including Egypt to the South, Assyria to the North, and Persia to the East. Alexander's motto of *"there is nothing impossible to him who will try"* paid off because he never ended up losing a battle in his life![5] The four heads of the leopard likely represent the division of the kingdom of Greece into the four cardinal directions by Alexander's generals after his death.[6] However, even today, Greek culture has continued to thrive in philosophy, science, education, and art. In fact, the book of Revelation describes a similar beast kingdom that would

---

[5] https://www.history.com/topics/ancient-greece/alexander-the-great

[6] https://www.worldhistory.org/article/94/the-hellenistic-world-the-world-of-alexander-the-g/

look like a leopard at the end of time, therefore prophesying that the pagan Greek culture would continue its influence over God's people until Christ's coming (Rev. 13:2).

The Terrible Beast—Rome

The fourth beast Daniel saw in his dream was by far the most terrifying! It was different from the rest, possibly being a composite beast with characteristics of the Grecian leopard beast before it (Dan. 7:7). It had huge iron teeth, ten horns, and feet with nails of bronze that "devoured, broke in pieces, and trampled" God's remnant people (Dan. 7:19). Although the kingdoms of Medo-Perisa and Greece are later identified in the book of Daniel (Dan. 8:20-21), the name of this kingdom is never directly mentioned. However, history is quite clear as to whom it represents. It could symbolize no other than the iron kingdom of Rome which defeated Greece. However, just as Bible prophecy predicted, Rome absorbed the Greek culture, signified by its *bronze* nails (a reference back to Nebuchadnezzar's dream of the statue [Dan. 2:39-40]). This terrible Roman beast would relentlessly persecute Christians, spanning before and after the time of Christ, ruling with fervor, especially during the third century.

However, hundreds of years later, the iron teeth of Rome would be temporarily broken, but its bronze, pagan nails would continually claw at Christianity, becoming the foundation of postmodern society. Today, for example, the current superhero movies are likely based on pagan Greek gods. Many believe that Superman is the embodiment of Zeus; Batman is Hades; Aquaman is Poseidon, and Wonder Woman is Hera.[7] So the influence of Greek mythology is still alive and growing more popular by the minute in movie media!

---

[7] https://profoundadvices.com/what-marvel-characters-are-based-on-greek-mythology/

The Little Horn of the Roman Empire—the Papacy

Next, Daniel was shown the terrible beast's ten horns, specifically the little horn, that uprooted three others. This strange horn had "eyes of a man and a mouth speaking pompous words" (Dan. 7:8). This horn rose from the terrible beast of the Roman Empire after it was divided into several European nations. Its civil power would also be religious because it would blasphemy God, persecute His people, and "think to change times and law" (Dan. 7:8, 25). Moreover, the little horn had the eyes of a man (a religious leader [Is. 29:10]), a mouth speaking proud words (Dan. 7:8), and its appearance and influence were greater than the others (Dan. 7:20). Furthermore, throughout the Dark Ages, many faithful Christians would sacrifice their lives because of the mandates of this little horn, fulfilling the prediction that it would "war with the saints" and prevail against them (Dan. 7:21). Finally, through its own ecclesiastical authority, this little horn would attempt to transfer God's seventh-day Sabbath to the first day of the week. Also, it would delete the second commandment that prohibits bowing down to idols and encourage worship of the saints,[8] fulfilling the Bible's prophecy that it would "think to change times and law" (the Ten Commandments [Ex. 20:4-6, 8-11; Dan. 7:25]). History proves that only one political/religious power fits the description of this little horn. However, the Lord knew that many of His faithful people, including teens today, would have no idea of the identity of the little horn, so He sent them clues in the prophecies of His Word.

A New Nation Is Born

The Bible states that the power of the little horn would be interrupted after a "time, times, and half a time," when "judgment was

---

[8] https://www.beginningcatholic.com/catholic-ten-commandments; https://gracethru-faith.com/ask-a-bible-teacher/why-are-the-catholic-10-commandments-different/; https://www.vatican.va/archive/ENG0015/_INDEX.HTM

made in favor of the saints" (Dan. 7:22, 25, NKJV). Using the biblical day-for-a-year principle found in Numbers 14:34 and Ezekiel 4:6, three and a half times 360 days in a Jewish year equals 1,260 prophetic days or years. Since the papacy gained political power after defeating the Ostrogoths in 538 AD, 1260 years later ended in 1798, the same time Napoleon's general, Berthier, captured the pope. About that same time, a new nation was forming across the ocean—a nation based on religious freedom—the United States of America! This Protestant nation would offer the world a haven of protection from religious persecution for a time.

The Investigative Judgment Begins

After Daniel saw the symbols of Babylon, Medo-Persia, Greece, and Rome, his attention was drawn to a beautiful scene taking place in Heaven. He watched as Jesus, the "Son of Man" came to the "Ancient of Days," His Father, to begin judgment in the heavenly courts by opening and reviewing the books (Dan. 7:9-10, 13, 26). When did this event occur? This heavenly judgment must have begun after the fall of these four world nations and the little horn power, which would take place sometime after 1798 AD (when the pope was taken captive). Daniel was not given the exact starting date of the investigative judgment until a later vision. However, after the rise and fall of these four beast kingdoms, the investigative judgment would begin for God's people (Dan. 7:9-12).

Presently, we are living in the last days of this heavenly judgment for those who claim to be Christians (Rev. 14:7). However, we have nothing to fear! (Jude 24). The good news is that all of us can receive Christ's white robe of righteousness (Zech. 3:3-5; Rev. 3:5). You just must ask the Lord to cleanse your heart from sin and choose to have Him change you into His image (Ps. 51:2, 7-13).

Then He promises that He "is able to keep you from stumbling, and to present you faultless before the presence of His glory with exceeding joy" (Jude 24). In fact, Christians should be happy the investigative judgment is occurring right now because it means that soon Jesus will come, and sin will be destroyed forever!

Just like a giant chain of events, the world's history is constantly repeating the past and linking it to the future. With each repetition, time is spinning faster and faster like a penny in a spiral, hastening Christ's return when "… the greatness of the kingdoms under the whole heaven" will be "given to the people of the saints of the Most High" (Dan. 7:27, KJV). The pressing question today is: *Am I ready?*

DANIEL 2'S STATUE/IDOL	DANIEL 7'S BEASTS/KINGDOMS (Dan. 7:23)
Rise/Fall Nations Ruling God's People Throughout History (Dan. 2:21; 7:12, 14, 27; Eccl. 3:11, 14)	**The Great Sea ("yam"- "Mediterranean")** **Sea- populated** (Dan. 7:2; Rev. 17:15; Is. 17:12) Winds-strife; directions (Jer. 4:11-13; 49:36-37)
Babylon—Gold Head (Dan. 2:37-38) Head- King Nebuchadnezzar (Dan. 2:37-38) Gold- Israel/God's People (Lam. 4:1-2; Hag. 2:5, 8; Joel 3:5-6) Kings of East- God's followers (Dan. 11:44; Matt. 2:1)	**Lion—Babylon (Dan. 7:4; Jer. 5:6, 15; 50:43-44)** Lion- Judah (Gen. 49:9; Jer. 12:7-8, KJV) Wings- extremity (Dan. 7:4; Is. 8:8; Jer. 49:22) Eagle- swift devourer (Jer. 4:13; Deut. 28:49; Dan. 4:33; Hab. 1:8; Lam. 4:19; Hosea 8:1) Plucked- ("bald"-"marat") (Dan. 7:4; Micah 1:16) Stood/two feet- rulership (Dan. 7:4; Ps. 47:3) Man's heart- character (Dan. 7:4; Eze. 36:26-27) Last-day nation- like mouth of a lion (Rev. 13:2)

Medo-Persia—Silver Chest/Arms (Dan. 2:32)	Bear—Medo-Persia (Dan. 7:5; Lam. 3:10-11)
2 Arms- Medes/Persians (Dan. 2:32; 8:20; Jer. 51:11)	3 Ribs in teeth- Babylon, Lydia, Egypt (Dan. 7:5)
Silver- God's people (Mal. 3:3; Zech. 13:9; Hag. 2:9; Eze. 22:18-22; Jer. 6:30; Joel 3:5-6)	Raised on one side- Persian dominant (Dan. 7:5)
	Told to devour flesh- violent (Dan. 7:5)
Kings of the East- God/ followers (Matt. 2:1-2)	Persecutes Israel (Gen. 16:11-12, 20; 2 Chron. 7:16-17; Amos 5:18-19; Prov. 28:15)
Cyrus- God's anointed (Is. 45:1)	
Abraham's descendants- Ishmael/Esau (Gen. 25:12-16; 27:40; 28:9)	Last-day nation-like feet of a bear (Rev. 13:2)
Greece—Bronze/Belly/Thighs (Dan. 2:32)	Leopard—Greece (Dan. 7:6; 8:21; Jer. 5:6; 13:23)
Greek (Joel 3:5-6; Dan. 8:21)	4 bird wings-worldwide (Is. 8:8; Jer. 49:22)
Bronze/Iron united (Lev. 26:19; Dan. 4:15; Jer. 15:12; 6: 28; Deut. 28:23; Ps. 107:16; Is. 45:2; 48:4; Micah 4:13)	Spotted- symbol of sin (Jer. 13:23; Eph. 5:27)
	4 heads-4 generals (Dan. 7:6; Deut. 1:15)
Evolves into Byzantine/Roman Empire (Dan. 7:19)	Rulership of N, S, E, W (Dan. 7:6; Luke 13:29)
Change of leadership to Gentile West	Last-day nation- like a leopard (Rev. 13:2)

Rome—Iron Legs (Dan. 2:33)	Terrible Strong Beast—Rome (Dan. 7:7)
Bronze/Iron- Greek influence in Rome (Dan. 7:19)	Huge iron teeth/nails of bronze (Dan. 7:19)
Conquerors of God's people (Ps. 2:8-9)	Devours & breaks (Dan. 7:19, 23)
God's people- transfers from East to West Gentiles (Mal. 1:11; Is. 60:17)	Tramples God's remnant (Dan. 7:19)
	Different- composite (Dan. 7:7, 19)
	10 horns- ruling powers (Dan. 7:20, 24; 13:1)
	Terrible nation (Jer. 15:20-21; Is. 25:3; 29:5, 20)
Europe/USA— Iron/Clay/Feet/Toes (Dan. 2:33)	**Little Horn- Papacy (Dan. 7:7-8, 20; Zech. 1:19)**
Divided- partly strong/partly fragile (Dan. 2:41-43)	Rises from terrible beast with iron teeth (Rome)
Clay- Spiritual Israel/USA (Lam. 4:1-2; Is. 41:25; 45:9; Is. 64:8; Jer. 18:4, 6; Micah 5:8; Rom. 9:20-28)	Uproots 3 other horns (Heruli, Vandals,
	Ostrogoths wiped out by papacy [Dan. 7:7-8]
Divided kingdom/conquers nations (Dan. 2:42; Ps. 2:8-9)	Eyes like a man- Pope (Dan. 7:8; Is. 29:10)
	Speaks pompous words (Dan. 7:8, 25; 2 Thess. 2:3-4; Rev. 13:5-7)

Christ/Law—Stone/Mountain Kingdom	Investigative Judgment Starts
(Dan. 2:34-35, 45; Rom. 9:32-33; I Peter 2:4-10)	**(Dan. 7:10, 26; Mal. 3:1-3 Mal. 3:1-3);**
Jesus's kingdom based on His law (Zech, 12:3; Ex 24:12; 31:18)	Books opened (Rev. 22:19)
Crushes metal idol (world kingdoms [Dan. 2:35])	Ancient of Days- God the Father (Dan. 7:9-10; Is. 44:6-8)
	Son of Man- Jesus (Matt. 18:11)
Mountain fills the earth (New Jerusalem [Dan. 2:35; Dan. 9:16; Rev. 21:10])	Christ receives His kingdom (Dan. 7:14,27)

DISCUSSION QUESTIONS FOR DANIEL 7

1. What do "beasts" in Bible prophecy represent? (Dan. 7:17, 23)

2. How is the description of Nebuchadnezzar/Babylon like the description of the lion? (Dan. 7:4; Dan. 4:33; Jer. 50:43-44)

3. What kingdom is symbolized by the ferocious bear with three ribs in its mouth and raised on one side? (Dan. 7:5; compare Dan. 8:20)

4. What kingdom is represented by the leopard with four heads and four wings? What do the four heads and four wings symbolize? (Dan. 7:6; compare Dan. 8:21-22)

5. Describe the terrible beast kingdom. How was it different from the rest? (Dan. 7:7)

6. Describe the "little horn" on the terrible beast. Who and/or what does it represent? (Dan. 7:8, 24-25; 8:20-26)

7. Why shouldn't Christians be fearful of the judgment that is taking place currently in Heaven? What has Christ provided for His people? (Zech. 3:3-5; Jude 24; Rev. 3:5)

THE RAM, THE GOAT, AND THE LITTLE HORN

*"And he said, 'Look I am making known
to you what shall happen in the latter
time of the indignation; for at the appointed time the end shall be.'"*

(Daniel 8:19)

Have you ever watched baby goats and lambs play? Little lambs often run and frolic in fun, but baby goats are a whole different story! They butt each other and rough and tumble. They may even jump on their mother's back and ride her like a horse! If you're not careful, they might just butt you if you get in their way!

Daniel's Dream

In Daniel's second vision, he saw a ram and a goat, but they definitely weren't playing! The male sheep had two notable horns. One of its horns was higher than the other, and the higher one came up last. The ram was pushing toward the West, the North, and the South (meaning that it originated from the East where Abraham's descendants lived). No animal could stop it, and it did whatever it wished.

But suddenly, a male goat came from the West, so fast that it seemed not to touch the ground! This angry goat butted the ram with its one, gigantic horn that was between its eyes and trampled the sheep under its feet (Dan. 8:3-7).

This rough male goat grew so big and strong that its large horn broke into pieces, and in its place, four horns came up in four different directions. Out of the West, a little horn sprang up, growing great in the South, the East, and in the North, the Glorious Land where God reigns (Is. 14:13; Ps. 48:1-2). It grew so great that it reached the heavens, and it threw down some of the stars and trampled them. This little horn became so proud that it declared that it was greater than God, Himself! It cast down the Lord's sanctuary and the truths of God's Word, and no matter what it did, it just kept growing stronger and more popular! Then Daniel heard a voice ask, "When will God rescue His church and his people from being trampled by this little horn power?" And another voice replied that in 2,300 days, God's sanctuary would be cleansed (Dan. 8:8-14).

If you had had a dream like that, would you have been a little confused as to what it meant? Daniel certainly was! (Dan. 8:15). He must have realized that the beasts in this dream represented kingdoms as they had in his last vision (Dan. 7:23), except this time the animals were not wild, but sacrificial animals in the Lord's temple. Because of his Jewish background, he would have immediately associated these animals with the Day of Atonement, the judgment day, when God's sanctuary and people were cleansed from sin. Daniel may have also noted that the ram with one horn higher than the other seemed similar to the bear he had seen in his last dream that was raised up on one side. But other than that, he had no idea what the dream meant!

The Historical Ram and Goat

Fortunately, God sent an angel to interpret Daniel's vision. The angel told him that the ram in his dream symbolized the kings of Media and Persia (Dan. 8:20), but a change was coming! Although

Daniel's dream had occurred during the reign of Babylon's last king, Daniel would live to see Medo-Persia conquer Babylon a few years later. However, he would die before the "goat" kingdom of Greece would rise to power. Its notable horn between its eyes stood for its king (Dan. 8:21). This great horn was a symbol of Alexander the *Great,* the mighty Greek conqueror. However, when this mighty king would die, his kingdom would be broken into four smaller kingdoms. History proves the Bible right! Just as predicted, Alexander's generals divided the kingdom of Greece into four directions: to the North, Lysimachus took Thrace and much of Asia Minor; to the South, Ptolemy I ruled Egypt; to the East, Seleucus governed Mesopotamia; and to the West, Cassander controlled Macedonia and Greece.[9] God's people were spread out into these four directions. Even though the "goat" kingdom of Greece had ended, its pagan influence would continue to thrive throughout history.

The Little Horn

But who or what does the mysterious little horn represent? The little horn originated from one of the four directions of conquest in which the Greek kingdom was divided (Dan. 8:8-9). It rose from the terrible beast kingdom following Greece — the Roman empire, which absorbed the pagan Greek culture and evolved into papal Rome (Dan. 7:6-8, 19-20). Only one political and religious power fits the biblical description of this little horn power — the Roman Catholic papacy!

The pope would "exalt himself as high as the Prince of the host" (Jesus [Acts 5:31; Rev. 1:5]; Dan. 8:11, KJV]). He would claim the sovereignty of Christ on Earth (Dan. 8:11). Like Lucifer, the pontiff would exalt his "throne above the stars of God" ("stars"- a symbol of God's people [Dan. 12:3]) and claim to sit where God

9 http://www.fsmitha.com/h1/ch12dis.htm

sits, "in the sides of the north" (Is. 14:13, KJV). He would also "cast down some of the stars to the ground" (like Lucifer in Heaven [Rev. 12:4]), "trample them" (Dan. 8:10), and "destroy the mighty, and the holy people" (Dan. 8:24, KJV). The papacy would persecute God's remnant just like the terrible beast of pagan Rome from which it arose (Dan. 7:19-21), especially during the Dark Ages when millions of Protestants lost their lives for their faith. An army (the Swiss guard) would also be given to the little horn, and the pope would "cast truth down to the ground" and do "all this and prosper" (Dan. 8:12). "Through his cunning" he would "cause deceit to prosper under his rule," and he would exalt himself in his heart," and "destroy many in their prosperity" (Dan. 8:25). Finally, he would "even rise against the Prince of princes," but at Christ's coming, he would be "broken without human means" (Dan. 8:25). Only the papacy has fulfilled each of these descriptions throughout history by claiming to be God on Earth and trying to change the Ten Commandments by its own power.

How Long?

When Daniel realized that this little horn would persecute God's people and corrupt God's truth, he immediately wanted to know how long this power would last. The angel declared that God's sanctuary would be cleansed after 2,300 days. Now if these were just literal days, this time period would not be very long—only about six years, which would definitely not stretch to the "time of the end" (Dan. 8:17). So there had to be more than one way to calculate time in Bible prophecy! By carefully comparing scripture with scripture (Num. 14:34 and Ezekiel 4:6), God's people discovered that prophetic "days" could symbolize literal "years"; therefore, 2,300 days in Bible prophecy could represent 2,300 years. Unfortunately, the angel disappeared, and Daniel was left without knowing when the prophecy would begin. He would have to wait a long time before the angel would return and tell him the event that would signal its start.

The Ram and Goat of Today

However, Daniel was reassured that his vision referred to end-time events (Dan. 8:17) "in the latter time of the indignation," which would occur at an "appointed time" (Dan. 8:19). Therefore, his dream must contain a specific message for those of us living in the last days!

Kings of God's People

The angel identified the ram with the two horns in Daniel's dream as the *kings* of the Medes and Persians. Interestingly, God calls Cyrus, an ancient Persian king, His "anointed" because the Bible prophesies that he would issue the decree enabling the Jews to re-build the temple in Jerusalem (Is. 45:1). However, ultimately, *Jesus* is God's "anointed," the true Builder and King of His people (1 Sam. 12:12). Presently, the Lord is constructing His sanctuary in His children's hearts through the power of the Holy Spirit (1 Cor. 3:16). Soon, God will defeat Satan and rule forever upon the new earth (Rev. 21:1-5). So, the Father, the Son, and the Holy Spirit are the *true* Kings of God's people!

The Ram—Christ Our Sacrifice

Moreover, the ram or lamb is a common symbol of Christ and His death on behalf of mankind. In the book of Genesis, God substitutes a ram/lamb for Isaac as a burnt offering, signifying that man's sin would be transferred to Jesus (Gen. 22:8, 13). Christ is the sacrificial Ram/Lamb, not only for Isaac but for all of God's people (Jn. 1:29). This symbolism was also portrayed in the sanctuary service, especially on the Day of Atonement, when a ram was offered as a sin offering (Lev. 16:3, 5; 1 Pet. 1:18-19). However, at the cross, Christ gave His life to fulfill the requirements of the law, and since then, no more sacrifices have been required (Matt. 27:51; Heb. 10:19-20). Today, Jesus is in the heavenly sanctuary making atonement for sin as our High Priest (Heb. 10:19, 21). Christ's mediation and sacrifice for our sin are further illustrated in the book of Revelation when all of Heaven and Earth sing: "Worthy is the Lamb who was slain to receive power and riches and wisdom and strength and honor and glory and blessing!" (Rev. 5:12). In Revelation, the word, "lamb," is used twenty-seven times to describe Jesus (Rev. 5:6)[10]. Therefore, a ram/lamb may represent Christ and His mediatory work and sacrifice on our behalf.

Horns of the Ram

Furthermore, the Old Testament refers to God's people as rams and lambs (Jer. 50:8, 17; Is. 40:11). John applies the same word for lamb to describe Christ's disciples in John 21:15. Additionally, Revelation also refers to a beast (kingdom [Dan. 7:23]) coming out of the earth, having "two horns like a lamb," which represents a nation founded on the principles of Christianity (Rev. 13:11, KJV). So a ram or lamb appears to either represent Christ or His followers.

The Goat—Satan and His Followers

In contrast, the *Complete Jewish Bible* refers to the male goat as symbolizing the king of Greece (Dan. 8:21). Who might a Greek represent in the Bible? The New Testament uses the term, "Greeks," to refer to Gentiles (Col 3:11; Gal. 3:28; I Cor. 10:32). So, the king of Greece could also symbolize the king of the Gentiles. Then what might this male goat represent today? This Hebrew phrase refers to the goat used for the sin offering in the temple service (2 Chron. 29:23), but the word, *"sa iyr,"* used in Daniel 8:21 and 2 Chronicles 29:23 for a male goat(s), can also be translated as *"devil"* or *"demons,"* as it is in Lev. 17:7. Even today, a goat's head is one of the main symbols of the occult.[11]

---

[10] https://biblehub.com/topical/l/lamb.htm
[11] https://www.spiritualsatanist.com/essays/satanism/baphomet-why-goats-are-sa-

Likewise, this same symbolism of Satan and his kingdom was acted out in the sanctuary service on the Jewish Day of Atonement. The high priest would lay his hands upon the head of the scapegoat and confess over its head the sins of God's people. Then it would be released alive to wander in the desert (Lev. 16:8-10, 21-22), representing the Devil's responsibility for sin and his destiny of wandering the desolate earth for a thousand years after Christ's second coming (Rev. 20:1-3). Jesus also used goats as a symbol of the wicked who are cursed and thrown into the eternal fire prepared for Satan and his angels (Matt. 25:41). So, this goat symbol in Daniel 8 could very well be a representation of Satan and his Gentile kingdom (the goat), warring against Christ and His followers (the Ram).

The Great War Between Christ and Satan

Daniel's vision in chapter eight, then, is likely a figurative picture of the great spiritual war between Christ's followers and Satan's throughout history. Just as the Bible predicted, the Lord's people sacrificed their world leadership to the Western pagan Greek and Roman kingdoms, and God's people (the Ram's kingdom) were left under the "goat's" political rulership. Daniel 8 specifically focuses on the goat's papal "little horn" and its persecution of Christ's followers throughout the Dark Ages (Dan. 7:8, 25; 8:9-12). Furthermore, the prophecy predicts that the Lord's sanctuary would be cleansed after 2,300 days, and the persecution of God's people would then end for a time (Dan. 8:13-14). Although Daniel was not shown when the 2,300 days would occur until later, Gabriel did assure him that the goat's little horn (the papacy) would finally be broken (Dan. 8:25). Christ's "ram" kingdom would be given a rest from the rulership of this goat's little horn. However, prophecy warns that the pope's power would rise again at the end of time (Rev. 13:1-7).

tanic.html

35

Today, one can see this return of the papacy's influence, even within the United States. Yet, the Bible promises that it will finally be destroyed at Christ's second coming, and after a thousand years, Satan and his hosts will be forever annihilated (Matt. 25:33, 41; Rev. 20:2-3, 7-10; Mal. 4:1, 3; Eze. 28:14, 18-19). The Lord pledges salvation for His people from the Devil and his followers in Zechariah 9:13, 16:

> For I have... raised up your sons, O Zion (ram), against your sons, O Greece (goat), and made you like the sword of a mighty man.... The Lord their God will save them in that day as the flock of His people. For they shall be like the jewels of a crown, lifted like a banner over His land.

Although many might see the signs of the papacy's comeback and the continual loss of countless religious freedoms in the world today, God's Word confirms that the Devil and his captives will, at last, be defeated. Praise God that the Ram, Christ and His kingdom, are promised to win in the end!

DISCUSSION QUESTIONS FOR DANIEL 8

1. What do the historical ram and its two horns represent, according to the Bible? (Dan. 8:3-4; 20)

2. What does God's Word teach about the historical goat and its great horn? (Dan. 8:5, 21)

3. How does prophecy describe the "little horn?" (Dan. 7:8, 20-21; 8:9-12) How has the papacy fulfilled the description of the "little horn?"

4. Who does the Bible symbolically refer to as the Ram/Lamb? (Rev. 5:6, 12; Jn. 1:29; Gen. 22:8,13; 1 Pet. 1:18-19)

5. Who else could the ram/lamb and its horns symbolize? (Matt. 25:31-33; John 21:15; Jer. 50:6-8; Is. 40:11; Eze. 34:17, 21-22)

6. Who might the symbol of the goat represent today? (Matt. 25:32-33, 41)

7. How does the sanctuary service on the Day of Atonement symbolize the goat's (Satan/the wicked) eventual destruction? (Lev. 16:22; Rev. 20:1-3, 7, 10)

8. What time prophecy, given to Daniel in this chapter, left him perplexed and why? (Dan. 8:14)

9. What assurance is given to us today as part of God's "Ram/Lamb" kingdom concerning the outcome of the war between Christ and His people and Satan and his followers (the goat)? (Zech. 9:13, 16)

SUSPENSE OVER

"So teach us to number our days, that we
may gain a heart of
wisdom."

(Ps. 90:12)

Have you ever read a book or watched a movie that left you hanging in suspense at the end? Likely, your immediate response was to get the sequel as soon as possible so you could find out what happens! Perhaps this is how Daniel felt after his vision in chapter 8. He had been left hanging following his last vision, and he knew that he needed help understanding the time period of the 2,300-day prophecy. So, he did what we still need to do now—he fasted and prayed, and the Lord heard his prayer! (Dan. 9:3). God sent Gabriel to give Daniel the "sequel" of his vision (Dan. 9:22-23), just as He will answer our request for wisdom to understand His prophecies today! (James 1:5). Lovingly, Jesus promises to give us His Holy Spirit who will show us "things to come" (John 16:13).

How Long, Lord?
Daniel desperately wanted to know the mystery of when to start the 2,300-day prophecy. If he had this clue, he could figure out the closing date of when the sanctuary would be cleansed and judgment would begin (Dan. 8:13-14; compare 7:10). He knew that the 2,300 days could represent 2,300 years in Bible prophecy by using the day-for-a-year principle found in Numbers 14:34 and Ezekiel

4:6. Because he stated in Daniel 10:1, "… the message was true, *but the appointed time was long,*" he understood that the vision of the 2,300 days would span a lengthy period of time but he had to know its starting date! In answer to his prayer, Daniel was given the event that would signal its beginning: "the *going forth of the commandment* to restore and build Jerusalem" (Dan. 9:25). Although the Bible records three such decrees (Ezra 1:1-4; 6:3-12; 7:11-25), the first two focused on rebuilding the temple, whereas the third decree of 457 BC included building Jerusalem's actual city structure in fulfillment of Daniel 9:25: "… *the streets shall be built again, and the wall,* even in troublesome times" (compare Ezra 6:14, 7:11-26, 9:9; Neh. 2:17; 6:15-16).[12] This was the key that Daniel had been looking for! Now that he knew the starting date, he could figure out the length of time God's truth would be trampled, and the sanctuary would be cleansed. This prophecy would end in 1844 AD,[13] the same period in history that the United States would rise as a world nation!

The Time of the End

Daniel could not have foreseen just how important this prophecy would become in the last days. However, a few years before the close of the 2,300-day/year prophecy (Dan. 8:14), William Miller, an American Baptist preacher, along with others, discovered its great significance.[14] Unfortunately, although they got the timing

---

12 https://biblearcheology.org/abr-projects-main/the-daniel-9-24-27-project-2/4589-the-going-forth-of-artaxerxes-decree-part1;
https://www.whitehorsemedia.com/docs/The-Commandment-to-Rebuild-Jerusalem-JN-Andrews.pdf
13 To figure the historical 2,300-day/year prophecy, you must begin at 457 BC and proceed 2,300 years. However, because the years before Christ's birth count backward, 457 years must be subtracted from 2,300 years, which ends in 1843 AD. Then another year must be added because there is no year 0 when changing from BC to AD. Therefore, you arrive in 1844 AD.
14 https://en.wikipedia.org/wiki/William_Miller_(preacher)

right, the event was wrong! They thought that Jesus would come back at the end of the 2300-day prophecy and cleanse the earth (the commonly accepted definition of the sanctuary at that time). However, they later discovered that on the Day of Atonement, falling that year on October 22, 1844, Jesus moved from the Holy Place to the Most Holy Place in the *heavenly sanctuary*, beginning His work of judgment of God's people (Dan. 7:9-14; Heb. 8: Heb. 8:1-2; 9:24, 27; 10:30). Christ's mediatory work as the High Priest in the heavenly temple would cleanse the hearts of God's people from sin during the investigative judgment, sealing them by His Spirit for the day of His return (Heb. 10:19-23; 2 Cor. 1:21-22).

Jesus and His Followers Are Given a Kingdom

Fortunately, the persecution of God's people by the papacy finally ceased in 1798, and the papacy lost its political rule in Europe (Dan. 7:25). About that same time, the United States of America was being formed. This country would become the haven of religious freedom for the world! The prophet, Daniel, predicted that God the Father would give Jesus "dominion, glory, and a kingdom" (Dan. 7:14). This kingdom may also be inferred in Revelation 1:5-6 (KJV) when the text states that Jesus is the "prince of the kings of the earth… and hath made us kings and priests unto God and his Father." Although Christ's kingdom will ultimately be fulfilled at His second coming, God's followers would first prosper on Earth through the religious freedom provided in the United States, allowing a repetition of Deuteronomy 30:16: "The Lord your God will bless you in the land which you go to possess." God has indeed blessed the United States and made this country *"kings" of the earth*—politically, financially, and most of all, spiritually. However, with these privileges come equally as great responsibilities!

Christ's Warning to His Nation

Sadly, as America's commitment to God continues to diminish, change is coming quickly! Instead of heeding the Lord's voice through obeying His law, this country's leadership has largely turned its back on the spiritual heritage of its founding fathers. Jesus warns:

> But if your heart turns away so that you do not hear, and are drawn away, and worship other gods and serve them, I announce to you today that you shall surely perish; you shall not prolong *your* days in the land… (Deut. 30:17-18)

Repeating the same sad cycle as Israel of old, the United States, God's blessed and chosen nation for spreading Protestant Christianity to the world, is apostatizing, just as prophecy has predicted (Rev. 13:11-16), but a faithful remnant will remain until Christ's coming who will keep "the commandments of God and the faith of Jesus" (Rev. 14:12).

Our Response

Today, more than ever, we need to pray Daniel's prayer:

> O Lord, great and awesome God, who keeps His covenant and mercy with those who love Him, and with those who keep His commandments, we have sinned… O Lord, hear! O Lord, forgive! O Lord, listen and act! Do not delay for Your own sake, my God, for Your city and *Your people are called by Your name.*" (Dan. 9:4-6, 18-19)

Christ's followers living today are *"called by His name"* — Christians — after Jesus, Himself. Additionally, many live in a country that claims Christianity (the United States) — the city *"called by His name."* Therefore, teens today must choose to confess their sins and pay attention to the Lord's truth (Dan. 9:13). They must hide God's Word in their hearts, so they won't sin against Him! (Ps. 119:11).

The Seventy-Week Prophecy—Then and Now

After Daniel finished his heartfelt plea, God immediately answered his prayer by giving him one of the most astounding time prophecies in all of history! This prophecy would point to the *very year* that Jesus would die for the sins of the world! The coming of the Messiah had been the Jews' passionate desire for generations, and Daniel must have held his breath in utter amazement as Gabriel revealed the specific amount of probationary time "cut off" from the 2,300-day/year prophecy for the Jewish nation: "Seventy weeks are determined for your people and for your holy city" (Dan. 9:24). Then the angel gave Daniel the missing piece of the puzzle from his former vision—the starting point of the prophecy: "from the going forth of the commandment to restore and to build Jerusalem," which occurred in 457 BC (Dan. 9:25; Ezra 7:6-13). This tiny piece of information was the golden key to unlocking the future! Now anyone could use the Bible's prophetic timetable to figure out exactly when the Messiah would come!

Daniel understood that the vision of the 2,300 days must span a long period of time (Dan. 10:1); therefore, he knew that the seventy-week prophecy could not just refer to seventy literal weeks. The Hebrew word for "weeks" in Daniel 9:24 means *"a period of seven days or seven years."* The 70 weeks (70 x 7), then, could equal 490 years. The historical seventy-week prophecy would begin in 457 BC at the rebuilding of Jerusalem and its walls and continue 490 years to 34 AD. The historical 2,300-day/year prophecy and the seventy-week prophecy would begin on this same starting date because it is the only event given to signal the start of both. Moreover, Daniel refers to Gabriel as the one "whom I had seen in the vision *at the beginning,*" who had come to help him understand his former vision (Dan. 9:21-23).

The angel continued by stating that after "sixty-two weeks, the Messiah shall be cut off" (Dan. 9:26), and "until Messiah the Prince there shall be seven weeks and sixty-two weeks" (Dan. 9:25). If seven weeks are added to sixty-two weeks, the sum totals sixty-nine weeks of years. Then if this total is multiplied by seven, it equals 483 years. If 483 years are added to 457 BC (the date of the decree to rebuild ancient Jerusalem and its walls), one arrives in 27 AD. What happened at this very time? Jesus was anointed at His baptism and began His ministry on Earth in this *same year*! Shortly afterward, the Messiah would be "cut off, but not for himself" (Dan. 9:26).

Then the most earth-shattering part of the prophecy was given—the exact year that the Messiah would die for the sins of the world! Christ would "confirm a covenant with many for one week: but in the middle of the week He shall bring an end to sacrifice and offering" (Dan. 9:27). Jesus confirmed his covenant with His people at His baptism in 27 AD. Then in the middle of the seven-year "week," or three-and-a-half years later in 31 AD, Christ died in fulfillment of the law, ending the need for the sacrificial system in the sanctuary. At that same moment, the four-inch-thick curtain separating the Holy from the Most Holy Place was torn from top to bottom by an unseen hand, creating an "open door" for Gentiles, as well as Jews, to enter God's presence through Christ's sacrificial death for sin. In giving His life, Jesus was truly "cut off but not for himself" (Dan. 9:26).

Sadly, just as predicted in the prophecy, three-and-a-half years later in 34 AD, the Jewish leadership formally rejected Christianity at the stoning of Stephen, and the gospel commission switched primarily to the Gentiles. Amazingly, Gabriel gave Daniel the *exact dates* of Christ's baptism in 27 AD, His death on the cross in 31 AD, and the ending of the probationary time for the Jewish nation as a whole in 34 AD. Yet, when Jesus was born, according to Jewish tradition, the leaders of Israel had put a curse upon anyone studying the time prophecies found in the book of Daniel.[15] The Jewish people were forbidden to research when the Messiah would come and when their "appointed time" of being God's chosen nation would end! Perhaps if they had diligently studied these time prophecies, the Jewish nation as a whole would have recognized Jesus as the Messiah and not crucified their own King! This tragic fate was predicted years before it occurred in the historical seventy-week prophecy, a part of the 2,300-day prophecy.

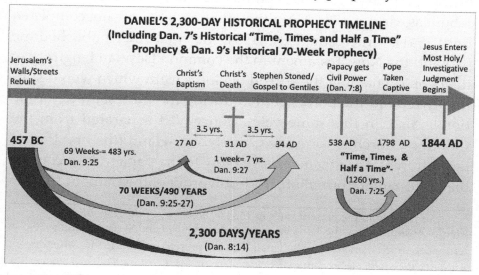

Double Trouble Today

Could it be that those of us living in the last days of Earth's history are seeing this prophecy repeated, and, like Israel of old, people living now are missing God's warnings that the United States is forsaking its designated purpose in spreading Christianity to the

---

[15] http://www.come-and-hear.com/sanhedrin/sanhedrin_97.html; https://amazingdiscoveries.org/AD-Header-Downloads-References-RabbinicCurse

world? The Bible says, "that which has been *is what will be done...* it has already been in ancient times before us" (Eccl. 1:9-10). Revelation 11:8 predicts that Jesus would be figuratively "crucified" by a modern nation in the last days. Many point to the French Revolution as a prime example of what happens to a nation when it forsakes God. Could this same rebellious spirit that caused so much tragedy be reoccurring in the U. S. today?

Once again, Daniel 9:25 states that at the command to rebuild Jerusalem, the seventy-week prophecy would begin. Has this decree ever been re-issued in modern times? Yes! Solyman the Magnificent, an Ottoman Turk, commanded that Jerusalem's walls be rebuilt as early as 1534 AD (although the walls were not completed until 1541).[16] Interestingly, in 1534, Martin Luther published the Old and the New Testament in the common German language of the people, enabling the spread of God's truth which would spiritually rebuild the Lord's church during the Protestant Reformation.[17] Also, in this same year, Henry VIII separated from the Catholic Church to form the Church of England (the first Protestant Church), striking a decisive blow to the papacy.[18] To counter the Protestant Reformation, the Jesuit order of the Catholic Church

---

[16] "...Solyman built the present walls in 1534." *Dictionary of the Holy Bible* by Charles Taylor; "Selim, the Turkish sultan, reduced Egypt and Syria, including Jerusalem, in 1517, and his son Solyman built the present walls in 1534." *Ruins of Ancient Cities; with General and Particular Accounts of their Rise, Fall, and Present Condition* by Charles Bucke, p. 379; "Selim, the Turkish sultan, reduced Egypt and Syria, including Jerusalem, in 1517, and his son Solyman built or reconstructed the present walls in 1534." http://biblehub.com/topical/j/jerusalem.htm; ATS Bible Dictionary

[17] Carl C. Christensen, "Luther and the Woodcuts to the 1534 Bible," *Lutheran Quarterly*, Winter 2005, Vol. 19 Issue, pp. 392–413

[18] https://www.parliament.uk/about/living-heritage/transformingsociety/private-lives/religion/collections/common-prayer/act-of-supremacy

was also established in 1534 AD, which would result in the death of countless Protestant martyrs.[19] All of these events occurred at the same time that Solyman decreed the rebuilding of Jerusalem's walls, possibly referred to in Isaiah 60:10, "The sons of foreigners shall build up your walls, and their kings shall minister to you." Could this event signal the repetition of Daniel 9's seventy-week prophecy for Protestantism and Christians living today?

Moreover, Solyman, this Ottoman ruler, was named after King Solomon, the builder of the original Jewish temple. Some historians have argued that Protestantism would have never succeeded in Europe without the financial aid of Solyman and the Ottoman Empire during this time in history.[20] So, the influence of this Turkish Sultan seems far more than just coincidental! If Daniel 9's prophecies were to repeat, and, for example, one begins figuring them in 1534 AD, the earliest date for Solyman's decree of the rebuilding of Jerusalem's walls, some amazing discoveries follow!

First, however, we must review the 2,300-day prophecy. Using the timing of a day-equals-a-year, we have already learned that the historical 2,300-day prophecy began in 457 BC with Artaxerxes's edict to rebuild Jerusalem and ended in 1844 when Christ moved from the Holy Place to the Most Holy Place to begin the investigative judgment. Since Christ cleansed the Jewish temple *twice* during His earthly ministry, both at the beginning *and the end,* it is logical that the 2,300-day prophecy of the cleansing of the sanctuary could repeat. Moreover, the 2,300-day prophecy in Daniel 8:14 uses two Hebrew words for the word translated as "day" — "*boqer,*" meaning "morning," and "*ereb,*" meaning "evenings." The text literally means, "Unto two thousand and three hundred *morn-*

---

[19] https://www.history.com/this-day-in-history/jesuit-order-established; http://www.alphanewsdaily.com/Number-of-Protestants-Killed-By-Popes.html

[20] https://www.jewishvirtuallibrary.org/suleyman

ings and evenings, then shall the sanctuary be cleansed." If we compare Daniel 8:14 to verse, 26, this prophecy seems to indicate that it may have more than one fulfillment: possibly in the "morning" for the Jews and in the "evening" for Protestants. If this prophecy were to repeat a second time, it must correspond to the seventy-week prophecy of Daniel. However, this time, instead of using a day-equals-a-year to calculate its duration, we will use God's method of timing found in Leviticus 25:8 and Deuteronomy 16:9. In Leviticus 25:8, the Lord instructs His people to count time in cycles of forty-nine years: "And you shall count seven sabbaths of years for yourself, *seven times seven years*; and the time of the seven sabbaths of years shall be to you *forty-nine years.*" This method of counting time in cycles of forty-nine years was a common practice for the Jews during the Second Temple era. Josephus, the Book of Jubilees, and the Dead Sea Scrolls all speak of the priests using cycles of forty-nine years.[21] Likewise, in Deuteronomy 16:9, God instructs, "You shall count seven weeks (sevens) for yourself...." The Hebrew word for "weeks" in this text can mean *seven days or years*. This is the same Hebrew word found in Daniel 9:24-27 for the word, *"weeks,"* which could refer to either *weeks of days or years*. Therefore, if we **multiply** 2,300 days by seven sevens (forty-nine), the total is 112,700 days. Then if these 112,700 days are divided by 365 days in a year,[22] the quotient comes to 308 years. If these years are added to 1534 AD, it brings us to the time period of the "Midnight Cry" of the Millerite Movement. This method of calculation of the 2,300-day prophecy simply reaffirms the former day-year method, largely repeating the last part of the historical

[21] https://www.jstor.org/action/doBasicSearch?Query=Once+again%2C+the+jubilee
[22] 360 days of a Jewish year are used in historical time prophecies & 365 (365.25) days are used in a modern year for the repetition of prophecies applying specifically to the Protestant era. The Bible does not specify either but likely uses both, depending on the time period and the audience.

2,300-day/year prophecy. It likely serves as a second witness, heralding the beginning of the investigative judgment and its urgent importance for God's people!

Concerning the seventy-week prophecy, then, the Bible states in Daniel 9:25, "Know therefore and understand that from the going forth of the command to restore and build Jerusalem... there shall be *seven weeks* and sixty-two weeks...." This verse gives further evidence that this time prophecy is likely being counted in seven-week (7 X 7) or forty-nine-year increments. Unlike the 2300-*day* prophecy, however, the seventy-week prophecy is figured in weeks of *years* instead of mere days. Therefore, one should not multiply by forty-nine because the seventy weeks are already in forty-nine-year cycles. Additionally, the prophecy states that there will be a total of sixty-nine weeks (or 483 years) until "the street shall be built again, and the wall, even in *troublesome times*" (Dan. 9:25). After this, the *"Messiah shall be cut off..."* (Dan. 9:26). Astoundingly if we add sixty-nine weeks or 483 years to 1534 AD (when Solyman decreed the rebuilding of Jerusalem's walls), we come to the year of 2017.

Amazingly, this is the very same year that Protestants and Catholics compromised on the doctrine of justification, purportedly ending the Protestant Reformation. Most Christians would agree that up to 2017, even in "troublesome times" (Dan. 9:25), God's truth, specifically the pivotal Protestant doctrine of justification by faith in Christ alone, marched steadily forward. But in 2017, everything changed! In that very year, the Lutherans, and many other mainline Protestant denominations, officially united back with the Catholic Church upon the doctrine of justification, the very same doctrine which had previously begun the Protestant Reformation.[23] This shocking compromise resulted in the combi-

---

[23] http://www.romereports.com/en/2017/07/15/reformed-churches-join-catholics-and-lutherans-on-the-doctrine-of-justification/

nation of the doctrine of justification by faith and the doctrine of salvation through works, purported by the pope. Moreover, Daniel 9:26 may further emphasize this tragic union between the Protestants and the papacy by predicting that "the people of the prince who is to come shall destroy the city and the sanctuary." This destruction spoken of in this prophecy likely includes the attack upon the biblical truth that we are saved by Christ's sacrificial death alone—not by penance or works we do ourselves.

Daniel 9:27 further expounds, "But in the middle of the week He shall bring an end to sacrifice and offering…." In the historical application of the seventy-week prophecy, the close of "sacrifice and offering" referred to the tearing of the temple curtain at Christ's death, ending the sacrificial system. Similarly, in this proposed modern repetition, in the middle of its last seven years (2020), could Protestant America have "cut off" or "crucified" Jesus afresh by nationally departing from His Word because of denying Christ's death on the cross as the only means of salvation (Rev. 11:8)? The prophet, Habakkuk, may have referred to this repetition of desolation when he cried out, "… Revive Your work *in the midst of the years! In the midst of the years*, make it known; In wrath remember mercy" (Hab. 3:2). Could Daniel's prophecy now warn that Protestant America, as a whole, has broken her covenant with God and judgments have begun to fall to awaken His people? Habakkuk also declares: "… before him went the pestilence (sickness)" (Hab. 3:5, KJV). Could the outbreak of Covid at this very time in history have been a wake-up call, warning the world of Christ's soon coming? One thing is certain, because of the global physical and economic devastation of Covid, plus the fires, storms, and violent protests, 2020 has gone down in history as unprecedented! Never before has the entire world been so engulfed in tragedy! (Hab. 3:6).

Also, in 2020, Pope Francis summoned the world's political, spiritual, social, and sports leaders to come together in unity under the pope's leadership. This call of the world's leaders under the pope's authority is likely a striking fulfillment of Habakkuk's prophecy: "... He is a proud man ... and he is like death, and cannot be satisfied. He gathers to himself all nations and heaps up for himself all peoples" (Hab. 2:5). Tragically, instead of Jesus, the pope has largely become the world's religious leader and his political power continues to grow in the United States, especially since Catholics now hold primary national offices, including the majority of the Supreme Court.[24] Could this transfer of spiritual leadership result in Christ's refusal of the unified apostate Protestant/Catholic churches, ending God's special protection and favor of the United States? (Jer. 14:12-13).

Daniel 9:27 continues by saying, "And on the wing of the abominations shall be one who makes desolate, even until the consummation (earth's closing events), which is determined is poured out on the desolate" (God's displeasure). Could the "wing" or ending of the repeated seventy-week prophecy (2024 AD) predict national devastations? Persecution of God's people? Even the conclusion of Protestant America as God's chosen nation similar to what occurred to the Jewish nation in 34 AD? Christ may have hinted at such a set time for national repentance when He told his disciples that they must forgive up to "seventy times seven," or 490 times, eerily like Daniel 9's 490-year prophecy (Matt.18:22; Dan. 9:24).

---

[24] https://news.gallup.com/opinion/polling-matters/391649/religion-supreme-court-justices.aspx

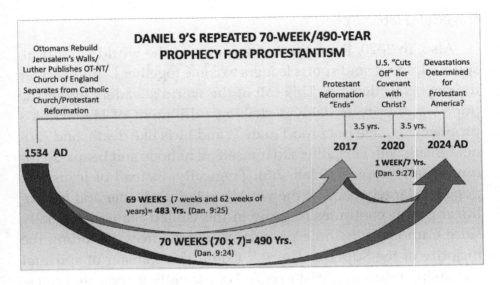

DANIEL 9'S REPEATED 70-WEEK/490-YEAR PROPHECY FOR PROTESTANTISM

Ottomans Rebuild Jerusalem's Walls/ Luther Publishes OT-NT/ Church of England Separates from Catholic Church/Protestant Reformation

Protestant Reformation "Ends"

U.S. "Cuts Off" her Covenant with Christ?

Devastations Determined for Protestant America?

3.5 yrs.   3.5 yrs.

1534 AD   2017   2020   2024 AD

1 WEEK/7 Yrs. (Dan. 9:27)

69 WEEKS (7 weeks and 62 weeks of years)= 483 Yrs. (Dan. 9:25)

70 WEEKS (70 x 7)= 490 Yrs. (Dan. 9:24)

An Alternative Application of the Repetition of Daniel's Seventy-week Prophecy

Another particularly fascinating way of figuring the repetition of Daniel's seventy-week prophecy is by using the starting date of 1541 AD, the completion of the restoration of Jerusalem's walls. Daniel 9:25 (KJV) states that the seventy-week prophecy would begin "from the going forth of the commandment ("debar" meaning "a word" or "oracle" [prophecy]) to restore ("shuwb" meaning "repetition") and to build Jerusalem." If one examines the meanings of the words closely, this text could be saying that from the time that the *prophecy* concerning the building of Jerusalem is *repeated*, the seventy-week prophecy would begin. Therefore, if we start the seventy-week prophecy on the ending date of 1541 AD when the walls of Jerusalem were completed, sixty-nine weeks (483 years) end in 2024, and seventy weeks end in 2031. The middle of the week (three and a half years added to 2024) would end in 2027, exactly 2000 years after the baptism of Jesus in 27 AD. Also, the ending date of 2031, is exactly 2000 years after Christ's death in 31 AD. Both dates were predicted in the historical seventy-week prophecy of Daniel 9, and the latter date likely ends 6,000 years of Earth's history.

Interestingly, the apostle Paul also states that God will finish His work upon the earth and *"cut it short"* (Rom. 9:28, KJV; italics added), which literally means to *"contract by cutting."* It may tie to the word, *"determined* in Daniel 9:24 (KJV) when God says that "seventy weeks are *determined* ("chathak"- "cut," "divided," "decreed")* for your people." Plus, it may mirror the description of the Messiah being *"cut off ("karath"- to covenant), but not for Himself,"* (Dan. 9:26, NKJV) which is further explained in the same verse as God's people breaking their covenant relationship with Him. Such parallels may indicate that the seventy-week prophecy is part of God's covenant with His people, applied to the Jewish nation and repeated for Protestants today. The repetition of this prophecy, then, should be a startling wake-up call for God's people living now!

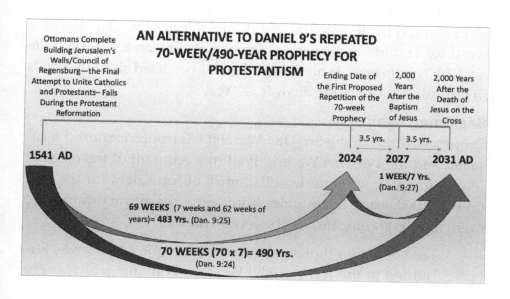

AN ALTERNATIVE TO DANIEL 9'S REPEATED 70-WEEK/490-YEAR PROPHECY FOR PROTESTANTISM

Ottomans Complete Building Jerusalem's Walls/Council of Regensburg—the Final Attempt to Unite Catholics and Protestants– Fails During the Protestant Reformation

Ending Date of the First Proposed Repetition of the 70-week Prophecy

2,000 Years After the Baptism of Jesus

2,000 Years After the Death of Jesus on the Cross

3.5 yrs. 3.5 yrs.

1541 AD   2024   2027   2031 AD

1 WEEK/7 Yrs. (Dan. 9:27)

69 WEEKS (7 weeks and 62 weeks of years)= 483 Yrs. (Dan. 9:25)

70 WEEKS (70 x 7)= 490 Yrs. (Dan. 9:24)

Regardless of the dates used to figure the repetition of the seventy-week prophecy, we must be aware of the times in which we are living, confess our sins, and live righteously *today* so that we will be prepared when Christ returns. Since the Bible does not give any prophecies predicting the date of Christ's second coming (*"but of the day and hour, no one knows..."* [Matt. 24:36]), we must pray for the Holy Spirit to help us understand and apply Bible prophecy to our lives NOW while there is still time!

Signs of Christ's Coming

As the end of time draws nearer, God's prophecies seem to be repeating faster and faster, like a coin spinning in a spiral! An additional application of the seventy-week prophecy has likely occurred recently. The Bible predicts the re-establishment of the Jewish nation as a sign for God's people. "This shall be a sign to you... the remnant who have escaped of the house of Judah shall again take root downward, and bear fruit upward. For out of Jerusalem shall go a remnant...." (Is. 37:30-32). Likewise, Daniel 9:25 may outline the timing of this prophecy by stating that the seventy weeks would begin with the rebuilding of Jerusalem. The Hebrew word for "build" is *"banah"* which can also mean to *"repair,"* *"to establish"* or *"to cause to continue."* Has this occurred since the 1500s in Jerusalem? Again, the answer is "Yes!"

Beginning Again

On June 7, 1967, in the Six-Day War, Israeli troops captured Jerusalem and the Western Wailing Wall (the remnant of the original Jewish temple), winning Israeli control of Jerusalem for the first time in 2,000 years. Testimonies from witnesses affirm this historic event and its significance to the Jewish nation:

> For some two thousand years the Temple Mount was forbidden to the Jews.... The Western Wall, for which every

heart beats, is ours once again…You have given the great privilege of completing the circle, of returning to the nation its capital and its holy center" (*Commander Motta Our to his brigade upon their recapture of Jerusalem's Old City and holy sites*).

I am speaking to you from the plaza of the Western Wall, the remnant of our Holy Temple… This year in Jerusalem — *rebuilt!* (General Shlomo Goren, Chaplain of the Israeli Defense Forces)[25]

On this date of June 7, 1967, the city of Jerusalem and its Wailing Wall were finally recovered for the Jewish nation as God had promised, "… I will bring back the captivity of Jacob's tents and have mercy on his dwelling places; the city shall be built upon its own mound…" (Jer. 30:18). Could this event begin a repetition of Daniel 9's prophecy?

In review, the Lord outlines the method of figuring time in Leviticus 25:8, "And you shall count seven sabbaths of years for yourself, *seven times seven years"* or "*forty-nine years."* Furthermore, as previously mentioned, Daniel 9:25 hints at counting in multiples of forty-nine years by referring to sixty-nine weeks of years as "*seven weeks* and sixty-two weeks." Applying this method to Daniel 9's seventy-week (490-year) prophecy and counting by forty-nine-year cycles like the Jewish priests, we discover that there are ten forty-nine-year cycles. If one of these forty-nine-year cycles is "cut off" (similar to the seventy-week prophecy cut from the 2300-day prophecy) and the Hebrew root words for the seventy-week prophecy are used, some amazing results follow!

For example, Daniel 9:24 states, "Seventy weeks are determined upon thy people and upon thy holy city…." If the root

---

[25] http://www.sixdaywar.org/content/ReunificationJerusalem.asp

word, "*sheba*," meaning "*seven*," is used instead of "*seventy*," this text would read, "*Seven* weeks (or *forty-nine years*) are determined ("*cut off*" from the seventy-week prophecy) for your people and your holy city." This method of figuring time, using a tenth of 490 years, or a forty-nine-year rotation based on the Hebrew root words, could then be applied to the sixty-nine weeks portion of the same prophecy. Daniel 9:25 states, "There shall be seven weeks and sixty weeks (equaling sixty-nine weeks) and after this, the "Messiah" would be "cut off, but not for Himself" (Dan. 9:26). As we have already discovered, Christ is the head of His nation, and when this prophecy is talking about the Messiah being "cut off," it could likely be talking about God's people in the Protestant nation of the United States being "cut off" from His spiritual leadership. If a tenth of sixty-nine weeks, 6.9 weeks, is multiplied by seven, it totals 48.3 years. Then if forty-eight years are added to the date that Jerusalem was "restored" to the Jews in 1967, the sum ends in the year 2015.

Did something significant happen in 2015 that would cause Christ's leadership of His Protestant church in the United States to be "cut off"? It was in this very year that the pope addressed the U.S. Congress for the first time in history. *But Daniel's prophecy is even more precise!* If the remaining .3 years are multiplied by 365 days, they equal 109.5 days. Then, if forty-eight years and 109 days are added to June 7, 1967 (the date that Jerusalem and the Western Wall were regained), we arrive on *September 24, 2015.* This is the *exact date* that Pope Francis spoke to Congress, advising the United States to join the Paris Agreement concerning climate change! [26] Never had a pope addressed the U.S. Congress in a formal session! The ancient prophecies found in Daniel 9, therefore, could give God's people today astounding insight into the timing

[26] https://www.theguardian.com/world/ng-interactive/2015/sep/24/pope-francis-addresses-congress-annotated

of when the pope would begin his rise to civil power, specifically in the United States. But why would Pope Francis urge U.S. leadership to unite with the world's nations in saving the planet through laws on climate control? This political consensus headed by the pope could give him powerful world leadership, which inadvertently might usher in compliance with his encyclical, *Laudato Si*, which promotes Sunday as the "day of rest."[27]

Heeding papal urgings, in December of 2015 (during the "middle of the week" [Dan. 9:27]), world leaders met in Paris to form a global pact on climate change.[28] A few months later, the U.S. Secretary of State, John Kerry, followed Pope Francis's advice by signing this climate covenant, along with 171 other world nations in April 2016.[29] Could this year also be predicted in Daniel 9's prophecies? If the root-word meaning of "seventy weeks" in Daniel 9:24 is used (seven sevens), forty-nine years may be added to 1967 which ends precisely in 2016, *the same year that the Paris Agreement was signed in alignment with Pope Francis' counsel!* This amazing application of prophecy is likely further explained in Daniel 9:27: "... and on the wing of abominations, shall be *one who makes desolate.*" Many are predicting a *devastating* impact on the U.S. economy because of the Paris Agreement.[30] Could it be that God's incredible prophecies, introduced in Daniel's visions and explained by John in the book of Revelation, are occurring now and are still in progress? Like a coin spinning in a spiral, these predictions seem to be repeating faster and faster with more and more precision!

---

[27] https://www.huffpost.com/entry/pope-francis-world-leader_n_56041e79e4b00310edfa4d0f; https://catholicecology.net/blog/laudato-si-day-praise-which-heals-our-relationships

[28] https://unfccc.int/process-and-meetings/the-paris-agreement/the-paris-agreement

[29] https://www.usatoday.com/story/news/world/2016/04/22/paris-climate-agreement-signing-united-nations-new-york/83381218/

[30] https://www.heritage.org/environment/report/consequences-paris-protocol-devastating-economic-costs-essentially-zero

Realizing that the prophecies of Daniel 9 are likely occurring in modern times compels us to pray more earnestly to "teach us to *number our days*," that we may gain salvation and not be deceived! Will we pay attention to the Bible's truth? (Dan. 9:13). Or will youth living today repeat the same sad history of ancient Israel and reject the prophetic warnings found in God's Word? Instead, may we pray for the Holy Spirit to help us heed the Lord's timely warnings through His prophets to prepare for His soon return!

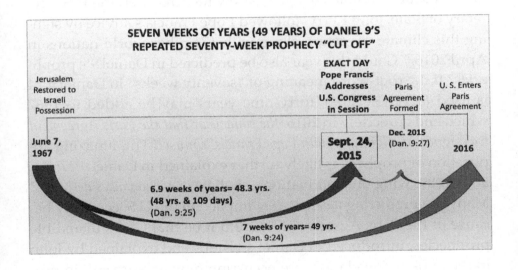

DISCUSSION QUESTIONS FOR DANIEL 9

1. What event signaled the beginning of Daniel's 2,300-day and seventy-week prophecies? (Dan. 9:25; Micah 7:11)

2. When Jesus moved into the Most Holy Place of the heavenly temple in 1844 at the end of the historical 2,300-day/year prophecy, what work did He begin? (Dan. 7:9-10; Heb. 8:1-2; 9:24, 27; 10:30)

3. Why is Christ's work of judgment so important for us living today? (Heb. 10:19-23; 2 Cor. 1:21-22)

4. What responsibilities do Christians have as God's people "called by His name?" How should this title affect our daily lives? (Dan. 9:18-19; Acts 15:17)

5. How many years did God give Israel as His chosen nation? (Dan. 9:24; Matt. 18:21-22)

6. In the historic seventy-week prophecy, what important event happened in 27 AD? (Dan. 9:25; Matt. 3:16) In 31 AD? (Dan. 9:26; John 19:30) What happened in 34 AD, and what did it signify? (Dan. 9:24; Acts 7:59; 13:46)

7. How might Ecclesiastes 1:9-10 support that Bible prophecies can apply to more than one event and time period in history? How did Christ teach this? (Matt. 24:1-3)

8. Why might the rebuilding of Jerusalem's walls in 1534 AD restart Daniel 9's seventy-week prophecy? (Dan. 9:25)

9. How did the unity of Catholics and Protestants "destroy" true Protestantism in 2017? (Dan. 9:26)

10. Why is it important to realize that prophetic dates refer to important **signs** of Christ's coming, **NOT** the **date** of His coming? (Matt. 24:36, 44)

11. Why is it important for our salvation to understand Bible prophecy, and how it applies to our lives right now? (Ps. 90:12; II Tim. 3:13-17)

SUPERPOWER

"You are of God, little children, and have
overcome them, because He who is in
you is greater than he
who is in the world."

(I John 4:4)

Have you ever wanted to travel through time faster than the speed of light with enough superpower to fight any enemy that might try to stop you? Daniel must have had a similar feeling when he realized his vision was true but "the time appointed was long" (Dan. 10:1). Interestingly, the Hebrew word for *"the time appointed"* means a great war. What long war had Daniel seen in his previous vision? It was the great controversy between Christ and His followers and Satan and his dark kingdom. This cosmic conflict is vital for all to comprehend because it is the backset of biblical prophecy. Everyone will choose a side in this deadly dual, and no one wants to be deceived!

The Bible predicts that the Devil will use a power that will speak "pompous words against the Most High," "persecute the saints," and try to "change times and law" (Dan. 7:25). Moreover, this leader will "destroy the mighty, and also the holy people, through his cunning," "cause deceit to prosper under his rule," and "exalt himself in his heart." Plus, he will "destroy many in their prosperity" and "even rise against the Prince of princes..."

(Dan. 8:24-25). As previously mentioned, only one power in history, rising from the Roman Empire, fits this description. It is the pope, the "little horn" power that "exalts himself as high as the Prince of the host" (Dan. 8:11). History has proven that the Roman Catholic system has persecuted and killed countless faithful Protestants throughout history and even today claims the Lord's divine authority. No wonder Daniel was distressed by the length of the terrible war by the papacy against God's faithful remnant!

In fact, Daniel was so upset that he mourned and fasted for three full weeks. The Bible emphasizes Daniel's fast in verse 3, *"I ate no pleasant food, nor meat or wine came into my mouth,* nor did I anoint myself at all, till three whole weeks were fulfilled" (Dan. 10:3). This fast was not some special diet plan that would merely benefit physical health! Instead, the purpose of Daniel's fast was to humbly confess his sins and the sins of his people and ask God not to "delay" in hearing his cry (Dan. 9:19). The fact that Daniel prayed and fasted is a powerful example for us today! This urgent call for prayer and fasting is desperately needed to obtain victory in the great controversy between good and evil because Jesus, Himself, declares that the Devil and his hosts sometimes cannot be overcome except "by prayer and fasting" (Matt. 17:21). Therefore, Christians today need the superpower of a radical prayer life to resist the evil forces striving to eliminate freedom of choice and gain the supremacy of the world!

Daniel knew the best way to stand for truth was to fight on his knees. He remembered God's amazing answer to his prayer when he was a teen and the king mandated that he and his friends had to eat the food that had been offered to idols. At that time, Daniel "purposed in his heart that he would not defile himself with the portion of the king's delicacies, nor with the wine..." (Dan. 1:8). Instead of complying with the king's mandate of what must be put into his body, Daniel and his three friends prayed and asked for a simple diet of vegetables (likely containing fruits and whole grains) and water for ten days. As a result, "God gave them knowledge and skill in all learning and wisdom; and Daniel had understanding in all visions and dreams" (Dan. 1:17, KJV). God honored their desire to keep their bodies as a "temple of the Holy Spirit" (I Cor. 6:19). Amazingly, when the king tested Daniel and his three friends, they were *"ten times better* than all the magicians and astrologers who were in all his realm" (Dan. 1:20). Interestingly, Daniel and his friends faced this health test first before they later faced the decree of forced worship that put Daniel in a lions' den and his three friends in a fiery furnace.

Similarly, the Lord will give today's teens wisdom regarding what they should put into their bodies and minds. Like Daniel, eating healthful foods and abstaining from alcohol and drugs will set God's followers apart from the crowd and make them ten times smarter than most of their peers! The Lord promises to give wisdom "liberally" to all who ask (James 1:5). Prayer, then, enables youth to make wise choices that not only improve their physical condition but also every other part of their lives!

As a result of Daniel's faithfulness in prayer, he was given a vision of the Son of Man like John's vision in Revelation 1. Both Daniel and John describe Jesus as being clothed in priestly attire of a robe with a golden belt (Dan. 10:5; Rev. 1:13). They also both describe Christ's eyes like torches of fire, his feet like fine brass, and his face shining with light (Dan. 10:6; Rev. 1:14-16; 2:18). These similar descriptions of Jesus seem to link the books of Daniel and Revelation together, explaining each other's prophecies, with specific relevance to the end of time. This description of Jesus, mediating in the heavenly sanctuary as our High Priest, gives us a tiny glimpse of the Lord's work for those who claim His blood as payment for the forgiveness of their sins (Rom. 8:33-34).

After Daniel saw Jesus ministering in the heavenly temple, the angel reminded him of the spiritual warfare that was taking place with the earthly rulers of Persia and Greece, a figurative description of the great controversy between Christ's followers and Satan's. In Daniel's day, the conflict between good and evil was particularly strong throughout the twenty-one days that Daniel fasted and prayed (Dan. 10:12-13), yet he was not discouraged by the evil forces that surrounded him!

Currently, with evil multiplying at unprecedented speed, all are called to follow Daniel's example of intercession as Christ's coming nears. The Lord promises to empower us just as He did when He touched Daniel and said, "… greatly beloved, fear not! Peace be to you; be strong, yes, be strong!" (Dan. 10:19). He reiterates this same promise and adds: "Fear not, for I am with you; be not dismayed, for I am your God. I will strengthen you; yes, I will help you; yes, I will uphold you with the right hand of my righteousness" (Is. 41:10). Praise the Lord that although the battle rages, we have nothing to fear with Christ on our side!

The details of this spiritual war between good and evil would be further outlined to Daniel in the future, but not before the angel assured him that Michael, his Prince, would win this fight against God's enemies. Jude 1:9 explains that Michael is the "archangel," meaning the "chief over all the angels" in Heaven, which is a reference to Jesus, Himself, called the "Angel of God" and the "Angel of the Lord" in the Old Testament (Ex. 14:19 compare 13:21; Judges 6:22-24). Therefore, Michael, the Prince, would give Daniel strength to overcome Satan and his hosts (Dan. 12:1).

The same superpower is available for Christ's youth today. Jesus has already won the battle with Satan at the cross. The Bible promises that by submitting to God, all can "resist the devil, and he will flee" (James 4:7). In addition, it states, "... greater is he that is in you, than he that is in the world" (1 John 4:4). Satan, therefore, is a defeated foe, and soon, Jesus will come and set up His kingdom on the recreated earth. Then, at last, this cosmic conflict will be ended, and good will triumph over evil once and for all!

DISCUSSION QUESTIONS FOR DANIEL 10

1. Why is it vital that we study prophecy in the context of the great controversy between Christ and Satan? How does awareness of this spiritual war protect us? (Eph. 6:12; Matt. 24:24; 2 John 1:7)

2. How did prayer help Daniel and his three friends? Why is it vital that we follow their example today? (Dan. 10:1-2; 9:3, 19; Joel 2:12-13, 28-29)

3. Why was it so important for Daniel and his friends to make wise decisions about their health? Why is it just as important for us to do the same today? (Dan. 1:8, 17, 20; I Cor. 3:16-17; 6:19-20; Matt. 17:18-21)

4. Compare Daniel's vision of the Son of Man to John's (Dan. 10:5-6; Rev. 1:14-16). How is Christ portrayed in both visions? Why is this description of Jesus significant in describing His current work in the heavenly sanctuary? (Heb. 9:15, 24; Rom 8:34)

5. What picture did God show Daniel in his vision of the great controversy between good and evil? How has God promised to protect us in this spiritual battle between Christ and Satan? (Dan. 10:13, 19-20; Is. 41:10; Rom. 8:31)

6. Who is Michael, and what does He do for God's people? (Dan. 10:21; 12:1; Ex. 14:19 compare 13:21; Judges 6:22-24; Jude 1:9)

7. How can we be prepared daily for the battle against the demonic influences in our lives? What promises are we given that we can overcome Satan through Christ's power? (Eph. 6:10-18; James 4:7; 1 John 4:4)

TWO KINGS, ONE PLOT

"Yet in all these things, we are more than conquerors through Him who loved us."

(Romans 8:37)

Have you ever played tug-of-war? If you have, you know that the object of the game is to pull the opposite team over to your side to win. Likewise, Daniel saw a figurative struggle between the King of the North and the King of the South in his last recorded vision (Dan. 10-12). Each king wanted to conquer the other, but amazingly, both end up on the same side, shaking hands under the table with a sly wink!

In Daniel's last recorded vision, the Lord traces the history of God's people to the end of time. Daniel 11:2 states, "Behold there shall stand up yet three kings (kingdoms- Dan. 7:17, 23) in Persia; and the fourth shall be far richer...." After the Achaemenid Empire (550–330 BC) which was in power when Daniel had his last vision, three more prominent, *strictly Persian*, dynasties arose—Sasanian Empire (224–651 AD), the Safavid dynasty (1501–1736 AD), and the Afsharid/Zand dynasty (ruling simultaneously, Afsharid: 1736–1796 AD/Zand dynasty: 1751–1794 AD). The fourth Persian kingdom was the Qajar dynasty (1796–1925 AD),[31] which was the richest, likely because of the discovery of oil in 1908 and the tremendous income it would produce. As a result, the West, namely the United States and Europe (including Greece, a member state

71

of the European Union), have today become dependent on Iran (Persia) for much of their oil. The resulting energy crisis has "stirred up" considerable political unrest in accordance with Daniel 11:2, "… and the fourth shall be far richer than them all; by his strength, through his riches, he shall stir up all against the realm of Greece" (Dan. 11:2), meaning that he would agitate all the realm of Greece or Gentile nations.

Next, the Bible recaps the Gentile history of Greece and Rome that was previously covered during the Persian Empires (similar to how Daniel 7 recaps Daniel 2's prophecy) by stating, "Then a mighty king shall arise, who will rule with great dominion, and do according to his will"; this kingdom would be "divided toward the four winds of heaven," and it would be *uprooted, even for others beside those*" (Dan. 11:3-4). History proves that Greece conquered Persia in 331 BC and was divided between Alexander's four generals. Then the Greek culture was absorbed into the Roman Empire and continued in the Catholic Church, illustrated in the conversion of the Greek gods into Catholic saints.[32] Daniel 8:23-24 expounds on the pope's rule in the Dark Ages by saying, "And in the latter time… a king shall arise, having fierce features, who understands sinister schemes…. He shall destroy the mighty, and also the holy people." This papal persecution occurred from the 14th to the 17th centuries during the Protestant Reformation.

During this time, faithful martyrs objected to the pope's highjacked authority of God who claimed to be "the Vicar of Christ,"[33]

---

[31] The Pahlavi dynasty ruled after the Qajar kingdom, but it is considered to be an Iranian kingdom because Persia became Iran in 1935. Then in 1979, Iran became a republic. Other ruling kingdoms throughout history were not considered strictly Persian. (https://en.wikipedia.org/wiki/History_of_Iran; https://www.britannica.com/place/ancient-Iran/Persian-dynasties; https://aspirantum.com/blog/persian-empire)

[32] Calvin, John. (1854). *A Treatise on Relics*. Edinburgh, Johnstone, and Hunter. p. 2

[33] https://www.papalencyclicals.net/leo13/l13praec.htm; https://www.nbcbayarea.com/news/national-international/Pope-Titles--196518461.html?amp=y

robbing the Lord of His kingdom in the rightful location of the North. This northern location was originally where God resided in the Holy Place of the sanctuary. Moreover, the Bible states that the "city of our God," "the great King," is in the North (Ps. 48:1-2, KJV). However, like Lucifer, himself, the papacy has exalted its "throne above the stars of God," claiming to sit "in the sides of the **north**" and be "like the Most High" (Is. 14:13-14, KJV). Also, the Bible describes the antichrist by stating, "he shall also stand up against the Prince of princes" (Dan. 8:25, KJV) and ascend from the iron and bronze kingdoms of Rome and Greece (Dan. 2:39-40), called "the **northern** iron and bronze" (Jer. 15:12). Therefore, in Daniel 11, the papacy is referred to as the self-proclaimed "king of the North."

The pope's political rulership over God's people would prevail until 1798 AD when the papacy would lose its civil power during the French Revolution. At that time, the papal authority would be "uprooted," in harmony with Dan. 11:4, and the king of the South "shall become strong, and one of his princes," and he would become more powerful than the king of the North and have great dominion (Dan. 11:5). However, the papacy would continue to fight for civil authority over God's people by spiritually attacking the king of the South.

Who is this king of the South that likely arose to world power after the papacy's fall in 1798? In Daniel 11, the king of the South is a symbol of a great nation containing God's people, symbolically located in the South (Dan. 11:8; Is. 30:1-6, 15; Eze. 16:46). It is further described in Revelation 11:8 as being spiritually called "Sodom and Egypt, where also our Lord was crucified." Similar to these ancient nations, this modern country is defiant against God like Egypt, known for its immorality like Sodom, and unfaithful to its spiritual vows like ancient Israel, crucifying Christ through its national apostasy. It is a country that claims to be Christian but has rebelled against God, legislated sexual miscon- duct, and idolized the lies of its apostate political/religious leaders. According to history, there is only one prominent Christian nation that arose to world power after 1798 that is fulfilling these specific characteristics today—the United States of America! The *king* of the South, then, would logically represent the United States' pri- mary national leader(s).

However, the prophecy does not end there. It continues in Dan- iel 11:6 by speaking of the king of the South's daughter that joins "together" and makes an "agreement" with the false king of the North (the papacy). What does this daughter symbolize? Ezekiel 23:2-3 states that God's people are *"daughters of one mother*—they committed harlotry in Egypt," *in the South* (Is. 30:3-7). Additionally, Ezekiel 16:46 declares, "to the *south* of you, is *Sodom and her daugh- ters."* So, when these texts speak of harlot "daughters" coming from "one mother," it appears to be occurring in the symbolic lo- cation of the South. As we have already discussed, the "South" may prophetically refer to the United States. Moreover, because a woman symbolizes a church in Bible prophecy (Jer. 6:2; Hosea 3:1; Eph. 5:23-32), these texts could be speaking of God's people resi- ding in "daughter" churches, specifically in the United States, that have become corrupted by "Mystery, Babylon the Great, the *Mother* of Harlots and of the Abominations of the Earth" (Rev. 17:5- 6). Only one modern entity asserts that it is the *mother church* of Christianity—the Roman Catholic Church! Who, then, would be its daughters? History has proven that the "daughters" coming from this "one mother" are the Protestant churches. So, the daugh- ter of the king of the South would logically refer to the apostate Protestant churches specifically located in the United States.

Tragically, many American Protestant churches have united back with their harlot mother, the papacy, who falsely claims to be the king of the North.

After understanding who is symbolized by the king of the North (the papacy asserting the authority of God) and the king of the South (the national leader(s) of the United States) and its spiritual daughter (the apostate American Protestant churches), one is prepared to study the rest of Daniel 11.[34] This prophecy likely outlines the history of God's people after the fall of the papacy in 1798 by introducing the king of the South: "Also the King of the South shall become strong, as well as one of his princes, and he shall gain power over him and have dominion. His dominion shall be a great dominion" (Dan. 11:5). Again, this text is likely referring to only one primary world-renowned nation during this period of history—the United States. After the fourth Persian kingdom ended in 1925, the United States of America rose to "unprecedented global power" following the World Wars.[35] However, the papacy was not to be left behind without a fight! The pope immediately began to rebuild his authority over God's people, this time specifically targeting his efforts in Protestant America.

In 1979, for the first time in history, Pope John Paul II met with U.S. President Jimmy Carter in the White House.[36] The pope also toured six American cities and was greeted by huge enthusiastic crowds; *Time* magazine, called him, "John Paul Superstar." This pope's popularity was a huge comeback to the political/religious power of the papacy in the United States. Later Pope John Paul II would work with U.S. President Ronald Reagan to bring down the

---

[34] Previous historic applications of the prophecies of Daniel 11 may also apply; however, the main thrust of this prophecy is "in the end of years" (Dan. 11:6, KJV).
[35] https://world101.cfr.org/historical-context/world-war/how-did-united-states-become-global-power
[36] https://time.com/4044254/pope-white-house-1979/

Iron Curtain of Communism.[37] Since then, this pope has been proclaimed to be one of the "most charismatic and influential religious leaders of the 20th Century."[38]

Moreover, his 1995 encyclical, *"Ut Unum Sint,"* strongly encourages interfaith dialogue united under papal leadership, [39]which is just what Daniel 11:6 predicts:

> ... At the end of years, they shall join forces, for the daughter of the king of the South (Protestant churches of the USA) shall go to the king of the North (the papacy) and make an agreement; but she shall not retain power of her authority, and neither he nor his authority shall stand, but she shall be given up, with those who brought her...." (Dan. 11:6, KJV)

If the daughter of the southern king represents the Protestant churches of America and the king of the North symbolizes the Roman Catholic papacy, then did American Protestants form an agreement with the Catholic Church? Yes! In 1994, a group of American evangelical leaders went to prominent Catholic scholars with the first major ecumenical document based on common points of doctrine called, *Evangelicals and Catholics Together.*[40] This agreement, signed by both evangelicals and Catholics, was a result of the interfaith dialogue that had begun in 1967, after the Second Vatican Council. Its principles would later become a benchmark

[37] https://www.usnews.com/opinion/articles/2015/09/24/ronald-reagan-pope-john-paul-ii-and-the-alliance-that-won-the-cold-war
[38] https://www.sfgate.com/news/article/POPE-JOHN-PAUL-II-1920-2005-Beloved-2718398.php
[39] http://www.usccb.org/beliefs-and-teachings/ecumenical-and-interreligious/resources/quotes-from-church-teaching-on-ecumenism-and-interfaith-dialogue.cfm
[40] https://www.latimes.com/archives/la-xpm-1993-06-22-mn-5726-story.html; https://www.firstthings.com/article/1994/05/evangelicals-catholics-together-the-christian-mission-in-the-third-millennium

of the Moral Majority in the 1970s.[41]

The Bible then states that a religious leader would arise from "a branch of *her* roots" (Protestantism), who would "enter the fortress of the king of the North (the Vatican), and deal with them and prevail" (Dan. 11:7). The spiritual warfare mentioned in this verse is likely symbolic of the conversion of many Catholics to Protestantism; moreover, this religious leader would "continue more years than the king of the North" (Dan. 11:8). Did a prominent American evangelist during this period of history convert many people, visit the Vatican, and end up living longer than Pope John Paul II? Yes! Billy Graham converted a staggering number of souls during his crusades—an estimated 2.2 million.[42] He also visited the Vatican in 1981 and 1990[43] and outlived Pope John Paul II by thirteen years.[44] His powerful influence on the evangelical ecumenical movement continues today.

Additionally, the visit by Pope John Paul II to the United States in 1993 resulted in stirring up strife between the U.S. president and the papacy over the issue of abortion,[45] as well as child abuse by the Catholic clergy in the United States.[46] This political conflict with the pope would grow until Bill Clinton was impeached in 1998.[47] Then, Pope John Paul II would return to the United States for his last time, possibly corresponding to Daniel 11:13, "For the

---

[41] https://oxfordre.com/religion/display/10.1093/acrefore/9780199340378.001.0001/acrefore-9780199340378-e-97;jsessionid=74B5C65BA06ECE3299F1A5D68F60A757

[42] https://factsandtrends.net/2018/02/21/billy-grahams-life-ministry-by-the-numbers/

[43] https://www.latimes.com/archives/la-xpm-1990-01-20-ca-221-story.html

[44] https://www.history.com/this-day-in-history/pope-john-paul-ii-dies; https://memorial.billygraham.org/official-obituary/

[45] https://www.nytimes.com/1993/08/13/us/pope-challenges-president-s-stance-on-abortion.html

[46] https://www.bbc.com/news/world-44209971

[47] https://www.congress.gov/congressional-report/105th-congress/house-report/830/

king of the North will return and muster a multitude greater than the former, and shall certainly come at the end of some years...."

His public appearance in the United States in 1999 drew a crowd of over 100,000 people at the St. Louis Trans World Dome for the January 27th mass—what is believed to be the largest indoor gathering in the United States.[48] This popular pope's historic visit had an astounding impact on Protestant America and paved the way for future ecumenical relations between Catholics and Protestants.

Daniel 11 continues its description of the false king of the North in verses 15-19 by stating that the armies "of the South" nor his "chosen people," shall have any "strength to withstand" him (Dan. 11:15). He will do "according to his own will and no one shall stand against him. He shall stand in the Glorious Land with destruction in his power" (Dan. 11:16). How did Pope John Paul II gain authority over spiritual Israel in God's modern "Glorious Land," the United States of America?

The following verse states that the king of the North would be given "the daughter of women (the Protestant churches) corrupting her..." (Dan. 11:17, KJV). Did something significant happen in 1999 between the Protestant churches of America and the Roman Catholic papacy? Yes! This is the same exact year that the historic *"Joint Declaration on the Doctrine of Justification"* by the Lutheran World Federation and the Catholic Church occurred.[49] This proc-lamation between the Catholics and the Lutherans would later climax in 2017 when many of the mainline Protestant churches would declare unity with the papacy on the doctrine of

---

[48] https://web.archive.org/web/20130616165933/http://www.ewtn.com/jp99/update.htm

[49] https://lutheranworld.org/what-we-do/unity-church/joint-declaration-doctrine-justification-jddj; https://www.ewtn.com/catholicism/library/joint-declaration-between-the-catholic-church-and-the-lutheran-world-federation-on-the-doctrine-of-justification-2290

justification, purportedly ending the Protestant Reformation.[50]

Daniel 11:18 continues, "After this he shall turn his face to the coastlands." Pope John Paul II returned to Italy's Mediterranean coast, and two years later, the United States would suffer one of the most devastating terrorist attacks in its history! On September 11, 2001, during the fall of the Twin Towers in New York City, "more than 2,600 people died at the World Trade Center; 125 died at the Pentagon; 256 died on the four planes.... This immeasurable pain was inflicted by 19 young Arabs acting at the behest of Islamist extremists headquartered in distant Afghanistan."[51] It would take ten years for U.S. forces to catch the mastermind behind this terrorist attack, but Osama bin Laden was eventually killed in a military raid on his compound hideout in Pakistan.[52] This terrible tragedy possibly correlates with Daniel 11:14: "Now in those times many shall rise up against the king of the South (USA). Also, violent men (i.e. terrorists) of your people shall exalt themselves in fulfillment of the vision, but they shall fall." As a result of this terrorist attack, the U.S. Patriot Act was passed, and many American constitutional rights were lost.[53]

Following the aftermath of this national tragedy, in 2005, Pope John Paul II died or would "stumble and fall, and not be found" (Dan. 11:19, KJV). His funeral would leave the world mourning and become one of the largest gatherings of world dignitaries in history up to that time.[54] Incredulously, the United States was represented at this pope's funeral by three American presidents—

[50] https://www.ncronline.org/news/world/reformed-churches-endorse-catholic-lutheran-accord-key-reformation-dispute

[51] https://govinfo.library.unt.edu/911/report/911Report_Exec.htm

[52] https://www.history.com/this-day-in-history/osama-bin-laden-killed-by-u-s-forces

[53] https://www.aclu.org/other/aclu-testimony-hearing-america-after-911-freedom-preserved-or-freedom-lost-senate-judiciary

[54] https://www.nytimes.com/2013/12/10/world/africa/nelson-mandela-south-africa.html?_r=0

George W. Bush, George H. W. Bush, and Bill Clinton—along with the secretary of state, Condoleezza Rice, and the New York mayor, Michael Bloomberg.[55]

Even after multiple court cases proving the guilt of child abuse by numerous Catholic priests in the United States under Pope John Paul II's papal rulership, this pope's "reproach" would "cease" (Dan. 11:18, KJV). In 2004, the American government passed a resolution that "commended the life and achievements of His Holiness, Pope John Paul II" after President Bush, with House and Senate support, gave him the Medal of Freedom.[56] However, the ample evidence of child abuse by the United States Catholic clergy would continue to haunt the papacy even after Pope John Paul II's death. Daniel 11:18 states, "… but a ruler shall bring the reproach against them (the Catholic Church) to an end, and with the reproach removed, he shall turn back on him." Astonishingly, American government officials chose to honor this pope despite the mountain of evidence of sexual abuse of minors found against Catholic clergy during his leadership.

After the death of Pope John Paul II, Pope Benedict XVI became the pope for eight short years. He criticized the United States tax havens for robbing the poor,[57] which is similar to the prediction found in Daniel 11:20, "Then shall arise in his place one who imposes taxes on the glorious kingdom…." Moreover, in 2013, for no apparent reason, Pope Benedict XVI resigned—something that had not occurred in the Catholic Church for almost six hundred years;[58] likewise, Daniel 11:20 states, "but within a few days, he

---

[55] https://www.washingtonpost.com/wp-srv/photo/pope/dignitaries/day.html

[56] https://www.congress.gov/congressional-record/2005/04/18/extensions-of-remarks-section/article/E678-2

[57] https://www.theguardian.com/world/2008/dec/07/pope-benedict-vatican-tax-havens-credit-crunch

[58] https://www.washingtonpost.com/local/pope-benedict-to-resign-citing-age-and-

shall be destroyed, but not in anger or in battle."

Daniel 11:21 continues: "And in his place shall arise a vile person to whom they will not give the honor of royalty; but he shall come in peaceably and seize the kingdom by intrigue." On March 13, 2013, Jorge Bergoglio became Pope Francis, replacing Pope Benedict in a peaceful transition. He is the first pope from the Americas and a Jesuit, an order of the Catholic Church formed in 1534 AD to oppose the Protestant Reformation. This Jesuit order was notorious for its cruel martyrdom of Protestants throughout Europe. According to John Wesley, by forty years after the beginning of the Protestant Reformation, more than *forty-five million* martyrs had been slain by the Jesuit Inquisition and other methods of Roman cruelty.[59]

Ironically, in direct contrast to his Jesuit vows, Pope Francis is known for his merciful teachings of helping the poor, the marginalized, and the neglected. Unlike his predecessors, he has purported a humble lifestyle by traveling in a Ford Focus, living in a Vatican guest house instead of the Vatican palace, and cooking his own meals. Furthermore, he is quoted as saying, "Call me Francis," and has been called the common "people's pope."[60] His reputation has gained him the title of "person of the year" by *"Time"* magazine and a nomination for the Nobel Peace Prize in 2014.[61] Notably, Daniel 11:21 predicts a religious leader whom "they will not give the honor of royalty, but he shall come in peaceably and

waning-energy/2013/02/11/f9e90aa6-743b-11e2-8f84-3e4b513b1a13_stor;
"Doctrine of Original Sin," Part I, section II.8, 1757, Wesley's Works, edited by Thomas Jackson, vol. 9, pp. 17-192

[59] http://www.alphanewsdaily.com/Number-of-Protestants-Killed-By-Popes.html
[60] https://poy.time.com/2013/12/11/person-of-the-year-pope-francis-the-peoples-pope/

[61] https://www.reuters.com/article/us-usa-pope-personoftheyear/pope-francis-named-times-person-of-the-year-idUSBRE9BA0JF20131211

seize the kingdom by intrigue."

Riding on a wave of unprecedented popularity, Pope Francis has pushed global political leaders, including those from the United States, to come into agreement on his socialistic agenda. He has vigorously opposed capitalism and economic inequality and urged governments to redistribute wealth.[62] In fact, Pope Francis has called capitalism the "dung of the devil" and blames it as "the underlying cause of global injustice and a prime cause of climate change."[63] Moreover, the pope urged former U. N. Secretary-General Ban Ki-moon "the world body must do more…" and encouraged the "legitimate redistribution of wealth,"[64] which parallels Daniel 11:39, "he shall cause them to … divide the land for gain." Furthermore, Francis declared "a just distribution of the fruits of the earth and human labor is not mere philanthropy. It is a *moral obligation*."[65] The pope's insistence aligns with Daniel 11:24:

> He shall enter peaceably even into the richest places of the province, and he shall do what his fathers have not done, nor his forefathers: he shall disperse among them the plunder, spoil, and riches; and he shall devise plans against the strongholds, but only for a time.

On September 24, 2015, Francis made history by being the first pope to address the United States Congress in a formal session. In this meeting, he urged U.S. national leaders to take immediate governmental action against pollution, climate change, and irresponsible consumerism. *The Guardian* summarized Pope Francis's

---

[62] https://www.washingtonpost.com/news/acts-of-faith/wp/2017/07/13/confidant-of-pope-francis-offers-scathing-critique-of-trumps-religious-supporters/

[63] https://www.nytimes.com/2015/07/12/world/americas/in-fiery-speeches-francis-excoriates-global-capitalism.html

[64] https://www.reuters.com/article/us-pope-un/u-n-should-encourage-redistribution-of-wealth-pope-says-idUSKBN0DP0WU20140509

[65] https://fortune.com/2015/09/14/pope-francis-capitalism-inequality/

appeal to Congress by saying that he had "laid out a bold vision of a more compassionate America which could use its might and ingenuity to heal the 'open wounds' of a planet ravaged by hatred, pollution, and inequality."[66] Interestingly, Bible prophecy predicts that a "wound" would be "healed," and "all the world" would follow the beast (Rev. 13:3). Evidence of the pope's worldwide influence became prominent just a few months later when over a hundred and eighty nations (including the U.S.) came together and signed the Paris Agreement concerning climate change.[67] This historic global pact was compliant with Pope Francis's second encyclical, entitled, *"Laudato Si, On Care of our Common Home,"* declared by the *New York Times* to be "one of the shrewdest documents issued by the Vatican during the past century" that "reveals Francis as a wily and sophisticated politician of the first order."[68]

When Pope Francis returned to the Vatican in 2015, after his historic speech to the United States Congress in formal session, he pushed Protestant, Islamic, Jewish, Orthodox, and a variety of other religious world leaders to unite on common points of faith. Pope Francis told 700 representatives of Islam, Judaism, and other faiths, "Religions, in particular, cannot renounce the urgent task of building bridges between peoples and cultures."[69] Moreover, he invited all to enter the "ark of fraternity," or, he warned, "there will not be a future."[70]

Tragically, in 2017, most mainline Protestant churches joined the pope's "ark of fraternity" by signing, *From Conflict to Communion,* a declaration of unity between the Lutherans and Catholics on

---

[66] https://www.theguardian.com/world/2015/sep/24/pope-francis-congress-speech
[67] https://unfccc.int/process/the-paris-agreement/status-of-ratification
[68] https://www.nytimes.com/2015/06/29/opinion/the-popes-ecological-vow.html
[69] https://www.americamagazine.org/faith/2019/02/04/pope-francis-worlds-religious-leaders-we-build-future-together-or-there-will-be-no
[70] ibid

the doctrine of justification, which some have claimed, ended the Protestant Reformation.[71] Daniel 11:22 expounds, "With the force of a flood they shall be swept away from before him and be broken and also the prince of the covenant." This flood imagery is also used in Revelation 12:15, "So the serpent (Satan [Rev. 12:9]) cast out of his mouth water as a flood, after the woman (church [Jer. 6:2]), that he might cause her to be carried away by the flood." This "flood" of unity, supported by Protestant leaders, was the result of the papal scheming that occurred in the 2016-2017 meetings of the Council of Cardinal Advisors, a small handful of influential leaders that Pope Francis appointed to guide him, likely aligning with Daniel 11:23: "And after the league is made with him he shall act deceitfully, for he shall come up and become strong with a small number of people." This "flood" of deception would sweep away the biblical doctrines of Christ's church through compromise.

Not all, though, have been supportive of Pope Francis's plans. Because of the wide differences still existing between Catholic and Protestant doctrines, some conservative religious leaders have accused Pope Francis of deceptive teachings by stating:

> ... the Roman Catholic Church's basic view of salvation, which is dependent on the mediation of the Church, the distribution of grace by means of its sacraments, the intercession of the saints, and purgatory, is still firmly in place, even after the Joint Declaration.[72]

They claim that neither side is correct in stating that the differences in their respective denominations have been reconciled, and

---

[71] https://www.ncronline.org/news/world/reformed-churches-endorse-catholic-lutheran-accord-key-reformation-dispute

[72] https://www.thegospelcoalition.org/article/is-the-reformation-over-a-statement-of-evangelical-convictions/

this unity does not represent the truth of God's Word.[73]

However, most of Catholic and Protestant leaders have applauded this interdenominational unity, ignored the doctrinal differences, and only highlighted the similarities. Pope Francis, himself, made a sweeping summary of this ecumenical event by stating, "Today, Lutherans and Catholics, Protestants, all of us agree on the doctrine of justification."[74] Similarly, the Lutheran World Federation's assistant general secretary, Dr. Kaisamari Hintikka, agreed, "The fact that all the historical churches of the west have now a shared understanding of justification is a wonderful way to mark the Reformation anniversary…. *What used to divide us, now actually unites us.*"[75] In stark contrast, Daniel 11:27 warns, "Both these kings' hearts shall be bent on evil, and they shall speak lies at the same table…. For the end will still be at the *appointed time.*"

Although the purpose of this Protestant/Catholic declaration was to bring peace and stability to all Christians, Pope Francis has openly declared his disdain for those who keep Christ's covenant (God's law [Jer. 31:31-33]). In fact, during a sermon delivered on January 27, 2017, in Casa Santa Marta, Pope Francis criticized "Christians who avoid taking risks out of concern for the Ten Commandments."[76] He claimed that these fundamentalists suffer from "cowardliness," warning that such people become "paralyzed," and are unable to "go forward."[77] Piggybacking on these

---

[73] ibid

[74] https://www.catholicnewsagency.com/news/full-text-pope-francis-inflight-press-conference-from-armenia-45222

[75] http://www.anglicannews.org/news/2017/10/lutherans,-catholics-methodists-reformed-and-anglicans-drawn-into-deeper-communion.aspx (italics added)

[76] https://www.lifesitenews.com/news/watch-pope-accuses-his-critics-of-coward-liness-for-overfocus-on-following-1

[77] ibid

statements, he also declared "Christians, who do not have the will to continue… who do not struggle for a change of things, for new things to come," fight against those changes which "would be a good for everybody."[78] He even went further by stating "religious fundamentalism must be combated. It is not religious, God is lacking, it is *idolatrous*."[79] These claims align with Daniel 11:28:

> While returning to his land with great riches (supporters), his heart shall be moved against the holy covenant (the Ten Commandments); so he shall do damage and return to his own land (Italy).

Moreover, Pope Francis accused religious fundamentalists of having the mental structure of "violence in the name of God."[80] While stressing that commandment-keeping Christians must abandon this brutal mindset, he declared "Muslim terrorism does not exist."[81] Likewise, Daniel 11 states that the king of the North would "corrupt by flatteries" those who "do wickedly against the covenant ([the Ten Commandments] Dan. 11:30, 32).

In contrast to his accusations against commandment-keeping Christians, Pope Francis has championed a dramatic positive change of attitude towards practicing homosexuals. When meeting Juan Carlos Cruz, the pope excused his gay lifestyle by stating, "It doesn't matter. God made you like this," echoing his former question concerning homosexuality, "Who am I to judge?"[82] Recently, Pope Francis has publicly supported same-sex marriages,[83] which,

---

[78] ibid

[79] https://www.ncronline.org/blogs/ncr-today/pope-francis-continues-his-critique-religious-fundamentalism

[80] https://www.catholicworldreport.com/2016/08/09/francis-and-fundamentalism/

[81] https://www.dailymail.co.uk/news/article-4237706/Muslim-terrorism-does-not-exist.html; https://cruxnow.com/vatican/2019/01/08/popes-outreach-to-islamic-world-in-2019-has-deep-roots/

[82] https://www.cnn.com/2018/05/25/world/pope-lgbt/index.html

along with the papacy's mandate of priestly celibacy, likely aligns with Daniel 11:37: "He shall regard neither the God of his fathers nor the desire of women, nor regard any god: for he shall exalt himself above them all."

What gives Pope Francis the right to make such astonishing unfounded statements? Perhaps one of the reasons for the world's rapt attention to his declarations is the fact that he claims to be the "Vicar of Jesus Christ" on Earth with the divine authority of Heaven itself.[84] Interestingly, Daniel 11:36 says: "Then the king shall do according to his own will; and he shall exalt and magnify himself above every god, and shall speak blasphemies against the God of gods, and shall prosper till the wrath has been accomplished: for what has been determined shall be done." The pope continues to "prosper," and his claim as Heaven's voice on Earth today goes largely undisputed. A plethora of voices now asserts that "among all the world's political and social leaders, Pope Francis stands increasingly alone as the most powerful force for global peace and stability."[85]

However, the Bible declares that the papacy will "honor the God of forces" (Dan. 11:38, KJV) and destroy the 'inherent, natural, and unalienable rights" of freedom of religion, such as found in the American Bill of Rights. In direct contrast to these efforts, the Word of God never supports forcing anyone against his or her conscience!

Also, Bible prophecy predicts that the papacy will gain political

[83] https://www.nytimes.com/2020/10/21/world/europe/pope-francis-same-sex-civil-unions.html

[84] https://www.nbcnewyork.com/news/national-international/Pope-Titles--196518461.html

[85] https://international.la-croix.com/news/the-radical-theological-vision-of-pope-francis/10477

power over the king of the South and its riches, even though Daniel 11:40 warns, "At the time of the end shall the king of the South (U.S.A.) attack him." The Hebrew word for "attack" in this text is *"nagach,"* which means to *"butt with horns."* This symbolism likely refers back to the larger conflict between the ram and the goat found in Daniel 8, which represents the great controversy between Christ's people (the ram) and Satan's (the goat). In the end, however, the papacy will be defeated, and Jesus and His remnant people will be victorious! Daniel 11:44-45 (KJV) promises:

> But tidings out of the east (where Christ returns [Matt. 24:27]) and out of the north (God's rightful kingdom location [Is. 41:25]) shall trouble him (the false king of the North [the papacy])... And he shall plant the tabernacles of his palace between the seas (people [Rev. 17:15]) and the glorious holy mountain (God's kingdom—spiritual Israel, specifically Protestant America [Dan. 9:15-20; Eze. 20:40; Micah 5:8]), *yet he shall come to his end, and none shall help him.*

Praise God that the historical accuracy of the Bible's prophecies can be verified, which gives us trust in His predictions that still lie in the future! One day soon, the papacy will be destroyed at Christ's second coming, and Jesus, the rightful King of the North, will win the final victory!

Daniel 11 contains many warnings against the deceptions of the papacy and its insatiable desire for control over Protestant America and the whole world. The question is: Will I pay attention?

DANIEL'S PROPHECIES SPANNING HISTORY

DANIEL 2	DANIEL 7	DANIEL 8	DANIEL 11
Head- Gold Nebuchadnezzar (**Babylon**/Jews) (605-539 B.C.)	**Lion** Eagle's Wings Plucked Stood/Man's Heart		
Shoulders/Arms Silver **Medo-Persia** (539-331 B.C.)	**Bear** Side Raised 3 Ribs in Mouth Told to Devour	**Ram** Medo-Persia Abraham's Seed God's Kingdom	3 More Kingdoms of Persia; Then 4rth Richer & Stronger
Belly & Thighs Brass- **Greece** (331-168 B.C.)	**Leopard** 4 Heads/4 Bird Wings Given Dominion	**Goat** Greece/Gentiles Satan's Kingdom	Mighty King Great Dominion Kingdom Divided into 4 & Uprooted (Greece)
Two Lower Legs Iron- Rome (168 B.C. – 476 A.D.)	**Terrible Beast** Iron Teeth/Brass Nails Ten Horns Tramples Remnant	From 1 of 4 Divided Kingdoms of Greece (Rome)	From 1 of 4 Divided Kingdoms of Greece (Rome)
Feet Iron & Clay **Papacy & USA** (476 A.D. - 2nd Coming)	**Little Horn** Defeats 3 Other Horns Wars Against Saints	**Little Horn** Sly, Proud King Destroys Saints (Roman Papacy)	**King of North** (Roman Papacy) **King of South** (USA)

DISCUSSION QUESTIONS OVER DANIEL 11

1. How is the history of Greece and Rome likely summarized in Daniel 11:3-4? (Compare Dan. 8:8)

2. Why does the papacy desire to be the "king of the North?" Who is the true "King of the North?" (Is. 14:13; Ps. 48:1-2)

3. Who is likely symbolized by the "king of the South" and further described in Revelation 11:8 as being **spiritually** called "Egypt, Sodom, and where our Lord was crucified?" (Dan. 11:5, 8; 42-43; Is. 30:1-2, 6-7 [Egypt]; Eze. 16:46; Lam. 4:6 [Sodom]; Lk. 23:28, 33; Heb. 6:3-6; [Jerusalem- where Christ was crucified])

4. Who may be represented by the "daughter" of the "king of the South?" (Dan. 11:6; Jer. 6:2 [woman- Zion/God's people]; Rev. 17:5 [mother- Mystery Babylon]; Eze. 23:2-3 [daughters])

5. What happened between the "daughter of the king of the South" and the "king of the North" that likely occurred in 1994? (Dan. 11:6)

6. What happened again in 1999 and 2017 that propelled the unity of Catholics and Protestants, and upon what doctrine did they unite? (Dan. 11:17)

7. What historic event in the USA likely corresponds to Daniel 11:14, and what was its effect on the rights of American citizens?

8. Why does Daniel 11:20 possibly parallel Pope Benedict XVI's resignation?

9. What specific disturbing characteristics has Pope Francis displayed that seem to parallel Daniel 11, verses 21? 23? 24? 28? 30? 32a? 36? 37? 38? 39?

10. What comfort are we promised concerning the final outcome of the **false** king of the North? (Dan. 11:44-45) What will the true King of the North (Christ) do when He returns? (Is. 41:25; Dan. 2:44-45, Rom. 8:37)

COUNTDOWN

"...Knowing the time, that now it is high time to awake out of sleep; for now our salvation is nearer than when we first believed."

(Romans 13:11)

"What time is it?" All of us have probably asked this question. Time is an intricate part of human life because our days are numbered—our time is running out! As Daniel watched the countdown of the last days of Earth's history (Dan. 10-12), he saw Michael (Christ), the "great prince who stands watch over the sons of your people..." arise to administer justice (Dan. 12:1). When Jesus went back to Heaven after His resurrection, He was *seated* at the right hand of His Father (Acts 2:34-36). However, when Daniel saw Christ *stand*, this posture signals the close of probation and the execution of judgment (Is. 3:13). Then, the Bible warns, there will be a "time of trouble such as never was since there was a nation" (Dan. 12:1).

This great time of trouble occurs when Jesus declares, "He who is unjust, let him be unjust still; he who is filthy, let him be filthy still; and he who is righteous, let him be righteous still; and he who is holy, let him be holy still" (Rev. 22:11). All the world's inhabitants will have made their decision—either to obey God and the everlasting law of His kingdom (The Ten Commandments [Ex.

93

20:1-17]) or Satan and his law of "Do what thou wilt."[86] Desolation of the earth from the seven last plagues will quickly follow this final pronouncement of judgment as Christ leaves His mediatory work in the heavenly sanctuary. However, Daniel is promised, "And at that time, your people shall be delivered, every one who is found written in the book" (Dan. 12:1 [Book of Life- compare Rev. 13:8; 20:15; 21:27]).

These words must have brought Daniel a measure of comfort, but he still longed to know more about the timing of these events. Then he heard a voice ask in Daniel 12:6, "... How long shall the fulfillment of these wonders be?" In answer to this question, Daniel saw "a man clothed in linen" above the water of the river who held up "his right hand and his left hand to heaven" and swore "by him who lives forever...." (Dan. 12:5-7). This is surely a reference to Christ, who had previously appeared between the banks of the river and instructed Gabriel to make Daniel understand the vision. Moreover, Daniel describes this "man clothed in linen" in nearly the same manner as John describes Jesus in the book of Revelation: "... One like the Son of Man, clothed with a garment down to the feet and girded about the chest with a golden band" (Rev. 1:13). John also records a similar location and actions in Revelation 10:5-6 when he writes of one standing upon the sea and the earth," who "raised up his hand to heaven and swore by Him who lives forever...." Moreover, this same body posture is found in Deuteronomy 32:40-43 when the Lord promises "vengeance to his adversaries" and "atonement for His land and His people." Only One of the Godhead could covenant with mankind by raising His hand in an oath, and Christ had been given this right by giving His life for humanity at the cross.

So, Jesus answered Daniel's question of how long by holding up His hands and swearing by Him that "lives forever that it shall

---

86 https://www.learnreligions.com/thelema-95700

be for a time, times, and a half a time; and when the power of the holy people has been completely shattered, all these things shall be finished" (Dan. 12:7). The Hebrew word for "completely shattered is the same word used in Daniel 9:27 for *"consummation"* "… and on the wings of abominations shall be one who makes desolate, even until the *consummation* …." This parallel may be a clue that Daniel 9's seventy-week prophecy ties to Daniel 12's time prophecies. This comparison will be further explored as we discover that Daniel 12's 1,290-day and 1,335-day prophecies likely end in the same years as the proposed repeated sixty-nine and seventy-week prophecies found in Daniel 9. Additionally, the seven weeks cut from Daniel 9's proposed repeated seventy-week prophecy appears to finish in the same year as Daniel 12:7's "time, times, and a half a time" prophecy.

Because the prophecies in Daniel 12 are some of the most mysterious ones in the entire Bible, one must examine carefully what Christ meant when He stated, "the power of the holy people" would be shattered after a *"time, times, and a half a time"* (Dan. 12:7). This timing *seems* to repeat the period mentioned in Daniel 7:25 that predicts the papacy's reign and its persecution of God's people:

> He shall speak pompous words against the Most High, shall persecute the saints of the Most High and shall intend to change times and law. Then the saints shall be given into his hand for a *time, times, and half a time.*

In this text, the Aramaic word for *"time"* is *"iddan,"* meaning a *"year."* If we use the historic day-for-a-year prophetic timing, 3.5 could be multiplied by 360 days in a Jewish year to get 1,260 days/years, which then could span from 538 AD to 1798 AD, the years that the papacy ruled politically in Europe.

However, the Hebrew word for "time" in Daniel 12:7 is "mow'ed." It is **not** the same word for "time" ("iddan") used in Daniel 7. It is instead the same word used in Daniel 8:19, 10:1, and 11:27, 29, and 35 translated as the **"appointed time."** It means a "fixed time or season," an "appointed meeting for a definite purpose," and "a signal or sign appointed beforehand." Because it does not mean a "year" like the word for "time" in Daniel 7:25, perhaps Daniel 12's prophecy could refer to a different time period and events than those found in Daniel 7. It seems to better fit the meaning of the "time, times, and half a time" prophecy in Revelation 12:14:

> But the woman (the church [Jer. 6:2]) was given two wings of a great eagle, that she might fly into the wilderness to her place, where she is *nourished* for *a time, and times, and a half of time* from the presence of the serpent." (Satan [Rev. 12:9])

The Greek word for "time" in this passage in Revelation is "kairos," meaning a "set time," "a fixed time," and "the decisive epoch waited for." This meaning of the word for "time" is nearly identical to the meaning of the Hebrew word in Daniel 12:7. Therefore, could this time prophecy refer to the same time period in the book of Revelation and coincide with a period of history when the church would be "nourished," and the "power of the holy people" would be "completely shattered" and "all these things" would "be finished"? (Dan. 12:7).

Back in Daniel 12:7, one can uncover an additional clue. The word, "mow'ed," refers to the "appointed time." Similarly, in Daniel 8:19, the Lord told Daniel, "Look, I am making known to you what shall happen in the latter time of the indignation; for at the **appointed time** *the end shall be.*" The word for "appointed time" is none other than the word, "mow'ed," the same Hebrew word for "time, times, and a half of time" in Daniel 12:7. According to Daniel 8:19, the "latter time of the indignation" would occur at the close of this time prophecy. The Hebrew word for indignation is *"za' am,"* meaning *"fury,"* especially of the Lord's displeasure with sin. By comparing Daniel 12:7, one can conclude that something would happen among God's people after a "time, times, and a half a time" that would make Him angry and propel the final events of Earth's history. Interestingly, in Jeremiah 8:7, the Lord mourns that His people do not recognize their "appointed times" for judgment. He cries: "Even the stork in the heavens knows her *appointed times* (*"mow'ed"*) ..." but my people do not know the *judgment* of the Lord." This text seems to associate the "appointed time" (*"mow'ed"*) with God's judgment, which began at the "cleansing of the sanctuary" predicted in Daniel 8:13-14. The time prophecies, then, in Daniel 12, would likely start at the close of the 2300-day prophecy in 1844, the beginning date of the investigative judgment. If these prophecies are calculated using God's method of timing found in Leviticus 25:8 and rotations of forty-nine years are figured like the Jewish priests of old, a "time" (forty-nine-years) would be added with "times" (two forty-nine-year periods equaling ninety-eight years) "and a half of time" (24.5 years), totaling 171.5 years (Dan. 12:7). Then, if 171 and a half years are added to 1844, the total comes to 2015. This is the same year that Pope Francis made his unprecedented speech to the U.S. Congress in formal session, and the papacy's political power significantly rose in the United States!

In his address to Congress, the pope urged the U.S. to join the world in taking immediate action on climate change and other social problems. Pope Francis stated:

> In *Laudato Si'*, I call for a courageous and responsible effort to "redirect our steps," and to avert the most serious effects of the environmental deterioration caused by human

activity. I am convinced that we can make a difference and I have no doubt that the United States – and this Congress – have an important role to play. Now is the time for courageous actions and strategies, aimed at implementing a "culture of care" and "an integrated approach to combating poverty, restoring dignity to the excluded, and at the same time protecting nature.[87]

The United States Secretary of State, John Kerry, followed the pope's counsel just seven months later on April 22, 2016, when he signed the Paris Agreement, along with over 171 other world leaders at that time.[88] Later, it was signed by President Obama before he left office.[89] This historic event, urged by Pope Francis, legally bound the United States in an official global pact with most of the world's leading nations concerning climate change. Not surprisingly, this pact has been reconfirmed by an executive order from President Biden,[90] who is Catholic.

Amazingly, Daniel 12's "time, times, and a half of time" prophecy can be figured even more precisely if one begins the 171 and a half years on the date of October 22, 1844, the actual ending date of the 2,300-day prophecy. If 171 years are added to October 22, 1844, this prophecy ends on October 22, 2015. Then if an additional six months are added, one arrives on April 22, 2016, the *exact day of the signing of the Paris Agreement!* This is also the same year that ends the seven weeks cut from Daniel 9's proposed repeated

---

[87] https://www.washingtonpost.com/local/social-issues/transcript-pope-franciss-speech-to-congress/2015/09/24/6d7d7ac8-62bf-11e5-8e9e-dce8a2a2a679_story.html

[88] https://www.cbsnews.com/news/us-climate-pact-un-signing-ceremony-paris-agreement-cop21/

[89] https://obamawhitehouse.archives.gov/blog/2016/09/03/president-obama-united-states-formally-enters-paris-agreement

[90] https://www.whitehouse.gov/briefing-room-/presidential-actions/2021/01/27/executive-order-on-tackling-the-climate-crisis-at-home-and-abroad/

seventy-week prophecy. Moreover, this type of world unity happening on this specific date in history has never occurred previously! One CNN commentator declared, "... the (Paris) agreement shows something that never has been apparent before: *The world is united on this issue.*"[91] More importantly, the world's alliance on climate change may have a far more reaching political and religious impact in the near future, and all of this may be happening in accordance with the timing of Daniel 12's prophecy!

Some might ask why the pope of Rome would be so interested in an agreement on climate change. Perhaps Pope Francis's own words in *"Laudato Si"* holds the key:

> Sunday, like the Jewish Sabbath, is meant to be a day which heals our relationships with God, with ourselves, with others and with the world. Sunday is the day of the Resurrection, the "first day" of the new creation, whose first fruits are the Lord's risen humanity, the pledge of the final transfiguration of all created reality. It also proclaims "man's eternal rest in God" ... The law of weekly rest forbade work on the seventh day (cites Ex. 23:12) ... And so the day of rest, centered on the Eucharist, sheds its light on the whole week, and motivates us to greater concern for nature and the poor.[92]

By encouraging Sunday-keeping as a "day of rest" that "motivates us to greater concern" for nature and the environment, Pope Francis has second-handedly encouraged the world to unite under his leadership in worshipping on Sunday, the first day of the week, instead of on Saturday, the seventh day, in direct opposition to God's fourth commandment that states: "*Remember* the Sabbath

---

[91] http://www.cnn.com/2016/04/21/opinions/sutter-paris-agreement-whats-next/

[92] http://w2.vatican.va/content/francesco/en/encyclicals/documents/papa-francesco_20150524_enciclica-laudato-si.html

day to keep it holy. Six days you shall labor and do all your work. But the *seventh day is the Sabbath of the Lord your God*" (Ex. 20:8-10).

The Lord, Himself, sanctified the *seventh-day Sabbath* as a memorial of creation and told us to *remember* it! (Gen. 2:2-3). Jesus and the apostle, Paul, also kept it holy (Lk. 4:16; Acts 18:1, 4). Moreover, not one verse in the entire Bible says that Christ changed the Sabbath to Sunday, the first day of the week! Instead, God's Word says that the Sabbath is the Lord's covenant (Is. 56:6), and He will not alter a word from His lips (Ps. 89:34) nor should one word be added or taken away from His commandments (Deut. 4:2). He outlines His covenant in Ezekiel 20, which refers to keeping His Sabbath day holy. Also, the Lord states "It is easier for heaven and earth to pass away" than for the smallest letter of His "law to fail" (Lk. 16:17). Furthermore, He declares "I am the Lord, I do not change" (Mal. 3:6); "If you love Me, keep My commandments (Jn. 14:15).

However, Daniel 7:25 warns us about one who would *"intend to change **times** (the Sabbath) **and law** (the Ten Commandments)."* Daniel 8:19 gives a clue to God's reaction to the change of His "times and law" by stating that His anger would occur at the "appointed time" in the *"latter time of the indignation."* Based on these texts, God must not be pleased with what happened in 2015-2016 when the United States signed the Paris Agreement promoted by the Roman pontiff who proudly claims to have changed God's holy Sabbath and His Law (the Ten Commandments [Ex. 20:1-17]).

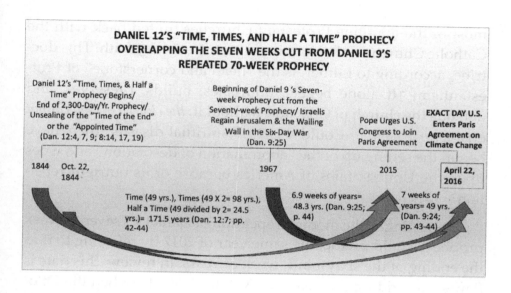

DANIEL 12'S "TIME, TIMES, AND HALF A TIME" PROPHECY
OVERLAPPING THE SEVEN WEEKS CUT FROM DANIEL 9'S
REPEATED 70-WEEK PROPHECY

Daniel 12's "Time, Times, & Half a Time" Prophecy Begins/ End of 2,300-Day/Yr. Prophecy/ Unsealing of the "Time of the End" or the "Appointed Time" (Dan. 12:4, 7, 9; 8:14, 17, 19)

Beginning of Daniel 9 's Seven-week Prophecy cut from the Seventy-week Prophecy/ Israelis Regain Jerusalem & the Wailing Wall in the Six-Day War (Dan. 9:25)

Pope Urges U.S. Congress to Join Paris Agreement

EXACT DAY U.S. Enters Paris Agreement on Climate Change

1844   Oct. 22, 1844

1967

2015

April 22, 2016

Time (49 yrs.), Times (49 X 2= 98 yrs.), Half a Time (49 divided by 2= 24.5 yrs.)= 171.5 years (Dan. 12:7; pp. 42-44)

6.9 weeks of years= 48.3 yrs. (Dan. 9:25; p. 44)

7 weeks of years= 49 yrs. (Dan. 9:24; pp. 43-44)

But Christ does not end His warning in Daniel 12 with the "time, times, and a half a time" prophecy. He also states in verse 11, "And from the time that the *daily* sacrifice is taken away, and the abomination of desolation is set up, there shall be one thousand two hundred and ninety days." This prophecy is said to have begun when the "daily" sanctuary offerings of the Holy Place were "taken away" (Dan. 12:11; 8:13; 11:31). When did this likely occur? As suggested earlier, it occurred at the close of the historic 2,300-day prophecy, when Christ moved into the Most Holy Place in 1844, ending the *"daily"* ministration in the Holy Place of the heavenly sanctuary (Dan. 7:9-14; Heb. 9:11-12; 24-25). Therefore, the 1290-day prophecy would likely begin in 1844, again giving further evidence of this starting date for the other time prophecies found in Daniel 12. Moreover, if seven weeks (49 days) are multiplied by 1,290 days (God's timing found in Deut. 16:9; compare Lev. 25:8), they total 63,210 days. Then if this total is divided by 365 days in a year, it comes to 173 years. If 173 years are added to 1844, the total comes to the infamous year 2017, the *very year* that most of the mainline Protestant Churches united back with the Catholic Church on the doctrine of justification by faith. This doctrine, according to Luther, is the "head and cornerstone" of Protestantism: "It alone begets, nourishes, builds, preserves, and defends the church of God, and without it, *the church of God cannot exist for one hour.*"[93] Could this 2017 spiritual disaster, then, have begun the setting up of the "abomination of desolation" and woes upon the United States of America because of its outright rebellion?

Interestingly, the modern repetition of Daniel 9's seventy-week prophecy could predict the same year of 2017 by referring to it as the ending of the sixty-ninth week of years. In review, this date is figured by adding 483 years (69 X 7) to 1534 AD (when the Ottomans commanded that Jerusalem's walls be rebuilt) which ends in 2017. Daniel 9 also speaks of "one who will make desolate" rising to power at the end of "abominations" (Daniel 9:27). Both Daniel 9 and 12 seem to predict this same year using *two different time prophecies* that refer to similar events which Jesus declares would happen at the end of time!

How did the Christian world set up this "abomination of desolation" in 2017? Protestant leaders united themselves with the papacy which has blatantly tried to change God's holy law and actively promotes that salvation is a combination of faith and works, specified by the traditions of the Roman Catholic Church. This stark difference from the original Protestant doctrine of justification by faith alone cannot be overemphasized! It was on this belief that Protestants originally separated themselves from the "mother" church and its "abominations" because they proclaimed that Christ gained man's redemption at the cross and good works could not earn salvation. Therefore, this controversial union on the doctrine of justification in 2017 has prompted many to declare that

---

[93] https://www.issuesetcarchive.org/issues_site/resource/archives/preus.htm

mainline Protestants have united back under the authority of the papacy and its unbiblical teachings, thus ending the Protestant Reformation.

Therefore, God, in His compassion for His people, has given us a roadmap that outlines the signs, specifically occurring at certain times, that would take place just before Christ's second coming. It is our duty as God's watchmen today to read and understand these prophecies found in the books of Daniel and Revelation so that we will not be deceived during these last days!

Unfortunately, like Daniel, we may be overwhelmed by God's timing and cry, "'Although I heard, I did not understand.' Then I said, 'My lord, what shall be the end of things?'" (Dan. 12:8). We are promised wisdom for this dilemma in Daniel 12:11: "Many shall be purified, made white, and refined, but the wicked shall do wickedly, and none of the wicked shall understand, but the wise shall understand." If we are willing to pray earnestly, we are promised that we *will* comprehend these prophecies. Christ will make them clear to all at the right time!

Daniel is told that a blessing is given to those who *wait* and come "to the one thousand three hundred and thirty-five days" (Dan. 12:12). Interestingly, Habakkuk was also told to wait: "for the vision is yet for an *appointed time ("mow'ed")*, but *at the end,* it will speak, and it will not lie. Though it tarries, *wait for it;* because it will surely come. It will not tarry" (Hab. 2:3). What were Habakkuk and Daniel supposed to wait for? It was for the "*appointed time*" or "*mow'ed,*" that would occur "*at the end.*" As previously shown, this same "appointed time" is referred to in Daniel 8:19, "... for at the *appointed time (mow'ed), the end shall be*" and Daniel 12:7's, "time ("mow'ed), times, and half a time." Likely these texts, then, point to a specific time in the end.

Since both Daniel 12:7's "time, times, and half a time" prophecy and Daniel 12:11's 1290-day prophecy likely began in 1844 when the daily sacrifice ended at the close of the 2300-day prophecy, it is logical to use this same starting date for Daniel 12:12's prophecy of the 1,335-day prophecy. Therefore, if 1,335 days are multiplied by forty-nine, they total 65,415 days. Then if this number is divided by 365 days in a year, it comes to 179 years. If one adds this time period to October 22, 1844 (the ending date of the 2,300-day prophecy), it ends in October of 2023. Amazingly, this is just before the close of the repeated seventy-week prophecy beginning in 1534 AD, the earliest command to rebuild Jerusalem's walls by the Ottomans and ending 490 years later in 2024.

According to this 1335-day prophecy of Daniel 12, God's people are promised that if they wait and stay committed to Him throughout this time, they will receive a blessing (Dan. 12:12). The apostle, Paul, states in the New Testament:

> Therefore, do not cast away your confidence, which has great reward. For you have need of endurance, so that after you have done the will of God, you might receive the promise: *"For yet a little while and He who is coming will come and will not tarry.* Now the just shall live by faith...." (Heb. 10:35-38)

This prophecy does not specify just what all this blessing entails, but God will soon reward His faithful followers and end the desolation of His church. We do not need to worry about whatever lies in the future because He has promised, "The Lord is on my side; I will not fear: what can man do to me?" (Ps. 118:6).

This promise was vividly illustrated when Daniel's three friends refused to obey the king's mandate of idol worship. Just moments before they were thrown into the flames, they boldly declared, "… our God whom we serve is able to deliver us from the burning fiery furnace, and He will deliver us from your hand, O king. But if not, let it be known to you, O king, that we do not serve your gods…" (Dan. 3:17-18). Amazingly, the king's soldiers dropped dead for simply getting near the furnace, yet the only thing that burned up on the faithful three Hebrews was their ropes! (Dan. 3:25). The fire that was supposed to have been their demise was instead the means of actually setting them free! Likewise, the Lord will free His followers today by pouring out the Latter Rain, giving them abundant power to witness to the world about His soon return.

Our prayer, then, should echo the Psalmist's: "Lead me in Your truth, and teach me: for You are the God of my salvation: On You do I wait all the day" (Ps. 25:5). May we stay ever faithful as we wait for the fulfillment of God's Word, knowing that the time for His return is near, even at the very door!

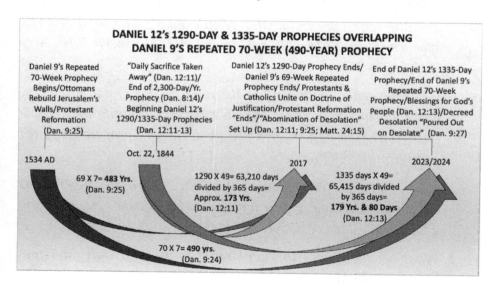

DANIEL 12's 1290-DAY & 1335-DAY PROPHECIES OVERLAPPING DANIEL 9'S REPEATED 70-WEEK (490-YEAR) PROPHECY

| Daniel 9's Repeated 70-Week Prophecy Begins/Ottomans Rebuild Jerusalem's Walls/Protestant Reformation (Dan. 9:25) | "Daily Sacrifice Taken Away" (Dan. 12:11)/ End of 2,300-Day/Yr. Prophecy (Dan. 8:14)/ Beginning Daniel 12's 1290/1335-Day Prophecies (Dan. 12:11-13) | Daniel 12's 1290-Day Prophecy Ends/ Daniel 9's 69-Week Repeated Prophecy Ends/ Protestants & Catholics Unite on Doctrine of Justification/Protestant Reformation "Ends"/"Abomination of Desolation" Set Up (Dan. 12:11; 9:25; Matt. 24:15) | End of Daniel 12's 1335-Day Prophecy/End of Daniel 9's Repeated 70-Week Prophecy/Blessings for God's People (Dan. 12:13)/Decreed Desolation "Poured Out on Desolate" (Dan. 9:27) |

1534 AD — Oct. 22, 1844 — 2017 — 2023/2024

69 X 7= 483 Yrs. (Dan. 9:25)

1290 X 49= 63,210 days divided by 365 days= Approx. 173 Yrs. (Dan. 12:11)

1335 days X 49= 65,415 days divided by 365 days= 179 Yrs. & 80 Days (Dan. 12:13)

70 X 7= 490 yrs. (Dan. 9:24)

DISCUSSION QUESTIONS FOR DANIEL 12

1. How can we deduce that the "man clothed in linen" that swore an oath is Jesus, not a common man or angel, and why would this be important? (Dan. 12:6-7; 8:15-16; Rev. 1:13; Duet. 32:39-40)

2. What promise does Christ make to the wise who study these prophecies? What should we do if we don't understand? What did Daniel do? (Dan. 12:3, 10; 9:3, 20-23)

3. When did the historical "time, times, and half a time" prophecy of Daniel 7:25 occur, corresponding to the period that the papacy ruled politically in Europe?

4. What happened at the end of the proposed repetition of the "time, times, and half a time" prophecy found in Daniel 12:7?

5. Why is the pope's urgency to fight climate change by resting on Sunday instead of God's seventh-day Sabbath in direct conflict with the Ten Commandments? What example did Christ and His apostles leave us? (Ex. 20:8-11; Deut. 4:2; Lk. 16:17; 4:16; Acts 18:4; Jn. 14:15)

6. What happened at the end of the repeated 1,290-day prophecy, likely concluding in 2017? Why is this year so significant to Protestantism? How does it correspond to Daniel 9's proposed repeated sixty-ninth-week prophecy? (Dan. 12:11; 9:25)

7. Although the Protestant nation of America may be in danger, what are we to individually wait for? (Dan. 12:12; Hab. 2:3; Ps. 25:5; 27:14)

8. What promises does the Lord make to all who wait on Him? (Is. 30:18; 40:31)

TIME'S UP

"And behold, I am coming quickly, and My reward is with Me, to give every one according to his work."

(Revelation 22:12)

Have you ever awakened to the insistent beeping of your alarm clock, hit snooze, and missed an important appointment? A warning is only good if the person receiving it pays attention!

Living in the twenty-first century, some might feel that the Bible is outdated or irrelevant, but nothing could be further from the truth! God's Word contains vital warnings for us today and a treasure full of promises. Specifically, the prophecies of Daniel predict what is happening *now,* and in the future, so none need to be deceived! Additionally, the book of Revelation projects an even greater picture of current events and their final outcomes! (Check out the sequel to this book entitled, *"Game Over, the Prophecies of Revelation Unsealed for Today's Teen).*

Will you take the time to study and understand these important truths? If you will, the hidden secrets of God's Word will never cease to amaze you! Christ will reveal His exciting plans for your life, and you will discover that His Word will guide you through difficult times. The Lord promises, "For I know the thoughts that I think toward you... thoughts of peace and not of evil, *to give you a future and a hope"* (Jer. 29:11).

God wants courageous youth who will spread the good news of Christ's soon return. You can be one of the Lord's, "called, chosen, and faithful" (Rev. 17:14), who keep the commandments of God and the faith of Jesus" (Rev. 14:12). Unlike unreliable preacher Joe, at the beginning of this book, who ran from his special calling and was absorbed in his worldly lifestyle, the Lord is urgently looking for faithful teens who will study, obey, and share the Bible's truths with others.

The world's clock is ticking, and time is running out! Just this past January, atomic scientists moved Earth's doomsday clock up to 90 seconds before midnight.[94]

At any moment, life could change drastically! Yet, we have nothing to fear! The Lord confirms that He will never leave God's followers or forsake them by promising, "I am with you always, even to the end of the world" (Matt. 28:20, KJV).

What will you decide today? If you want to commit your life to Christ right now and follow the teachings of His Word, why not pray this simple prayer?

> *Dear Jesus,*
>
> *Please fill my heart with the Holy Spirit and forgive my sins. I claim Your power to help me obey the commandments in Your Word. Show me how to understand and apply the Bible's prophecies to my life today, so I won't be deceived. Give me confidence in Your promises to face the future without fear and help me tell the world of Your soon return!*
>
> *In Your name,*
>
> *Amen*

---

[94] https://abcnews.go.com/US/2023-doomsday-clock-announcement-expect/story?id=96495463

By praying this prayer of consecration, you have just embarked on the most exciting journey of your life! The Lord promises to do more for you than you can even imagine or think! (Eph, 3:20). So what are you waiting for? Go and tell the world that Jesus is coming back and make your life count for Christ in these last days of Earth's history before—**TIME'S UP!**

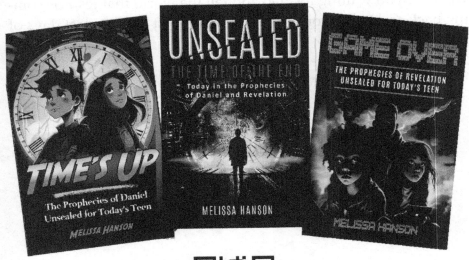

For the latest prophecy information and more books by this author, please visit unsealedthetimeoftheend.com

Made in the USA
Monee, IL
16 July 2024

61484720R00066